Lead with
PURPOSE
Make an
IMPACT

44 Lessons in Effective Coaching & Leadership

Other Works by Allistair McCaw

7 Keys to Being a
Great Coach

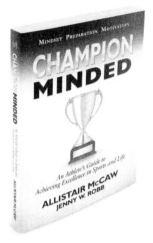

Champion Minded

Becoming a
Great Team Player

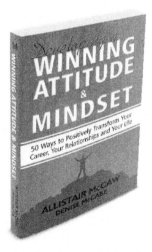

Developing a Winning
Attitude & Mindset

Purpose
The objective, aim or goal toward which one strives

Impact
The ability to leave a deep, desirable impression on another person

Lead with PURP⊙SE
Make an IMPACT

44 Lessons in Effective Coaching & Leadership

by
ALLISTAIR McCAW
DENISE McCABE

First Edition – November 2021

Published by Allistair McCaw

Allistair McCaw
M

www.AllistairMccaw.com

ISBN: 978-0-578-90697-3

Library of Congress Cataloging-in-Publication Data

Category: Self-Improvement, Leadership, Lifestyle, Mindset

Author: Allistair McCaw

Co-writer and Editor: Denise McCabe | www.MccabeEditing.com

Cover Design & Formatting: Eli Blyden Sr. | www.EliTheBookGuy.com

Printed in the United States of America by Book Bindery:
A&A Printing & Publishing | www.PrintShopCentral.com

Disclaimer

Contents

Other Works by Allistair McCaw iii

Disclaimer vii

Introduction 1

CHAPTER 1
Lead with Purpose 5

CHAPTER 2
Lead with Integrity 9

CHAPTER 3
Lead with Influence 13

CHAPTER 4
Lead with High Standards 17

CHAPTER 5
Lead with Self-Awareness 21

CHAPTER 6
Lead with Example 25

CHAPTER 7
Lead with Trust 31

CHAPTER 8
Lead with Vision 35

CHAPTER 9
Lead with Curiosity 39

CHAPTER 10
Lead with Care 43

CHAPTER 11
Lead with Authenticity 47

CHAPTER 12
Lead with Calmness 51

CHAPTER 13
Lead with Belief...55

CHAPTER 14
Lead with Adaptability...59

CHAPTER 15
Lead with Buy-In..63

CHAPTER 16
Lead with Humor..67

CHAPTER 17
Lead with Optimism...73

CHAPTER 18
Lead with Consistency 77

CHAPTER 19
Lead with Self-Leadership 81

CHAPTER 20
Lead with Compassion 85

CHAPTER 21
Lead with Communication Skills 89

CHAPTER 22
Lead with Healthy Confrontation.....................................95

CHAPTER 23
Lead with Vulnerability..101

CHAPTER 24
Lead with Open Mindedness..105

CHAPTER 25
Lead with Honesty..109

CHAPTER 26
Lead with Self-Confidence...113

CHAPTER 27
Lead with Collaboration...117

CHAPTER 28
Lead with Positivity..123

CHAPTER 29
Lead with Courage 127

CHAPTER 30
Lead with Connection 131

CHAPTER 31
Lead with Growth Mindedness 135

CHAPTER 32
Lead with Questions.. 139

CHAPTER 33
Lead with Commitment.. 143

CHAPTER 34
Lead with Humility 147

CHAPTER 35
Lead with Listening... 151

CHAPTER 36
Lead with Feedback 155

CHAPTER 37
Lead with Empathy 161

CHAPTER 38
Lead with Competence... 165

CHAPTER 39
Lead with Chemistry 169

CHAPTER 40
Lead with Appreciation... 173

CHAPTER 41
Lead with Energy 177

CHAPTER 42
Lead with Heart... 181

CHAPTER 43
Lead with Non-negotiables 185

CHAPTER 44
Lead with Impact... 189

Differences between a Poor Leader and a Great Leader .. 193

Conclusion 195

Lead with Purpose Workshop 197

About Denise McCabe 199

Introduction

Having been involved in the coaching and leadership worlds for well over two decades now, I have come across many coaches who were brilliant at the X's and O's but lacked good leadership skills. I have also come across many in the corporate world who were great at sales or marketing, for example, but when promoted to a management role, failed miserably to lead those under their wing.

Apparently destined for the career I'm in, whether I was a student in school, an athlete on a sports team or a professional in the sports or corporate world, leadership has always fascinated me. I am intrigued by how people lead and curious about why some leaders excel while others fail miserably. Why are some respected and trusted while others are not?

A great leader has two primary goals. The first is to accomplish either a personal or professional purpose, and the other is to have a positive, lasting impact on those they lead. A leader who works for only the first goal but doesn't care about the second is simply not great. What I have observed is that having a title, position or status doesn't, as some people believe, necessarily translate to being an effective leader. Correcting this misconception is one of my reasons for addressing the subject of leadership.

The example of the South African national cricket team, the Proteas, provided another motivation for writing this book. They had reached the number one position in world rankings three times over a ten-year period only to quickly lose it each time. Composed of men from very diverse backgrounds, they lacked a feeling of unity and a focused purpose. One day at a team meeting, team leader and captain Graeme Smith (a player I worked with earlier in his career) showed a video introducing the South African concept of ubuntu.

Ubuntu comes from a Zulu phrase that translates to "a person can be a person only through others": one can grow and progress only through the growth of others. From that day in 2010 to today, "Ubuntu" is the team's motto.

Moving to this side of the Atlantic, I discovered that NBA basketball coach Doc Rivers used ubuntu to pull the Boston Celtics team members together to win the NBA championship in 2008. Moreover, the words "A life is not important except in the impact it has on other lives. Ubuntu" are engraved on the tombstone of baseball Hall of Famer Jackie Robinson.

Because I grew up in South Africa, ubuntu speaks to me about the purpose of nurturing others and making a positive impact on their lives and growth. It inspired the title *Lead with Purpose, Make an Impact*.

When I meet leaders, one of the first questions I like to ask is "Why do you lead?" In fact, it's a question I'd like to pose to you. Why do *you* lead?

Having a deep-rooted objective is the starting point of great and effective leadership. If you don't know your purpose, you will be like a boat without a rudder—directionless. You won't know what route to take, which people you need to get onboard your team and possibly when, or even if, you have succeeded.

All of the great leaders I have had the pleasure of working with have had a compelling purpose. All are making (or have made) a lasting impact on those they lead by creating a deep connection with them, building their trust and earning the right to have an influence on them. This is where the line has been drawn between the good leader and the great one, the one who makes an impact.

The 44 lessons in this book illustrate how to rise to the level of greatness—how to achieve your goals and how to make a positive impact on those you lead. Each chapter defines practices of standouts in their fields and offers shrewd insights from many of them to guide the way for those who want to be among the best. At the end of each chapter are two self-reflection questions to help you become more self-aware. Use them to spark your own thoughts as well as discussion with members of your team.

Leadership is a learned and trained skill, not a given. In fact, a question I am often asked is "Are leaders born or made?" I believe it's a bit of both. Much the same as with an athlete, you need some genes, but you still need to put in the hard yards to better your skill set. If you want to be a great leader, you must first earn the necessary respect.

Great leaders give the best of themselves to get the best from their people. They are *their best selves* in order to inspire their people to be *their best selves*. Ubuntu. As the legendary UCLA basketball coach John Wooden noted, "Each member of your team has the potential for personal greatness; the leader's job is to help them achieve it."

Leadership isn't about rank or position; it's about achieving your goal and lifting others up. It is my hope that this book helps you to define your purpose, encourages you to be your best self and empowers you to make a fine and lasting impact on those you lead, including yourself!

Great leaders show up with Purpose.
Great leaders make an Impact.

CHAPTER 1

Lead with Purpose

I asked in the Introduction why you want to lead. Have you taken the time to formulate an answer?

It's a simple question and one of the first ones I ask anyone who's in a position of leadership. Funny thing is that you'd be surprised how many people have difficulty answering. The second question I ask is this: "How do you define and measure success as a leader?

Some might suggest that the purpose of a leader is to create a vision, set goals and find the right team members to achieve them. Some might suggest that it's to motivate and drive their people or to oversee daily operations. Some might suggest that it's simply to deliver results. Some might suggest that it's to inspire more leaders. None of these is incorrect. Leaders with purpose accomplish all of them, and more.

Of all the subjects we address in this book, the one that comes before the others is purpose. You can't lead with conviction if you don't know *why* you believe what you profess. You must know what leadership and success look like to you.

People want to follow a leader who is confident, who is resolute in their defined purpose and direction. They expect the person in charge to present goals to the team and clarify the path to the future. They count on their chief to excite them about the journey.

As a coach and leader, I have defined my purpose. It is to serve, impact and help others discover their own greater purpose and to empower them to live a life of meaning and fulfillment. I use writing books, keynote speaking, consulting and sharing content on social media as my means to lead with purpose and make an impact.

The purpose of a great leader goes beyond achieving certain organization goals. Patrick Lencioni, author of the book *The 5 Dysfunctions of a Team*, says that when he meets leaders or would-be leaders, the first question he, too, asks is "Why do you want to become a leader?" Knowing their motivation tells him a great deal about the likely quality of their leadership. Lencioni believes that there are two reasons why a person wants to become a leader. The first is the reward (position) and the second is the responsibility. A reward leader is interested in getting something for themselves, and the responsibility leader is interested in serving others. Great leaders are in the second group.

The best way to clarify your purpose is to stay connected to—or reconnect with—what is most meaningful for you. Ask yourself questions like

What is it that excites me about leading others?

What inspires me to keep going in the face of adversity or when difficult challenges strike?

What motivates me to continue leading others even when I feel as if everyone is against me?

When you answer these questions, you will have made a significant leap in understanding why you lead. Articulate your purpose. Then consider the other 43 characteristics we are examining—which ones you have and which still need to be developed.

Those who lead with purpose encourage their people, validate their efforts and celebrate their accomplishments and teamwork. They listen and learn. They are positive and encouraging. They set a straight and narrow ethical route for themselves and for their team members. And they have the abilities to be clear about these things and to smooth everyone's road to success. Whew! That is indeed a lot of responsibility!

Once you define the reasons why you lead, then your ability to understand your larger purpose becomes clearer. Great leaders don't lead simply because it's their job. They don't lead because they seek fame, power, money or attention. Great leaders lead to realize both their own vision and their greater purpose to inspire, empower and serve their people.

SELF-REFLECTION TIME

- ◎ What were the reasons you first wanted to become a leader?
- ◎ What is your defined purpose?

"Leadership is the capacity to influence others through inspiration, motivated by passion, generated by vision, produced by a conviction, ignited by a purpose."

– Dr. Myles Munroe

CHAPTER 2

Lead with Integrity

No great leader—and, in fact, no great person—lacks integrity. It is not just a feature of their reputation; it is woven into the fabric of their character. Real integrity is doing the right thing when nobody's going to know whether you did it or not.

Great leaders model integrity not only by doing what they say they'll do, but also by taking responsibility if things don't go well. Furthermore, having integrity means putting personal agendas aside to focus on the greater good of the organization, its people, and the people it serves.

Forbes magazine reports that in a business survey, integrity ranked higher than such leadership qualities as fairness, decisiveness, and stability. Among employees, 75 percent indicated that integrity is the most important attribute, although, interestingly, only 46 percent of CFOs held that opinion. What this implies is that, given a choice, people will leave an organization for more ethical (if not greener) pastures.

If you are aspiring to be a great leader in your organization, choose to demonstrate integrity. It generates respect, builds trust and validates credibility. The link between integrity and trust cannot be overestimated in the leader-team member relationship.

John Wooden, long-time head basketball coach at UCLA, placed high value on trust and credibility within his team. In fact, integrity was near the top of his famed Pyramid of Success. Coach Wooden said, "Make your 'yes' mean yes and your 'no' mean no." Even the players on the bench, who may have been frustrated by their lack of playing time, respected his standards and principles. One of those players, Andy Hill, still feels that this clarity allowed the UCLA teams to function at a higher level because everyone knew that Coach Wooden navigated with a moral rudder and was not playing favorites. Everyone knew their role on the team.

People will not be enthusiastic about following someone who has not first established their integrity and trustworthiness. Unfortunately, examples of poor integrity are too frequent. One example in recent sports history is Lance Armstrong, who was long admired as a cycling icon. He had claimed that anyone who said he was doping was lying, but it finally became obvious after several years of denial that he that he had used banned substances during all of his 7 Tour de France victories. In his effort to get people to look up to him as a cycling icon, he crashed and burned.

Leaders with integrity take the high road even if it is rough and in spite of the consequences. They readily admit when they are wrong because to deny mistakes, as with Armstrong, lays bare the ugly truth. Philanthropist and self-help book author W. Clement Stone advised, "Have the courage to face the truth. Do the right thing because it is right. These are the magic keys to living your life with integrity."

People with integrity are deeply committed to doing the right things for the right reasons, even when they are difficult or unpopular. Earn the respect of your team members, exhibit integrity and insist on it from them.

10 Examples of Integrity

1. You are honest about your shortcomings.

2. You take responsibility for your behaviors and actions.

3. You deal with conflict and confrontation respectfully.

4. You stand up for what's right.

5. You adhere to the values of your organization.

6. You give credit when it's due.

7. You don't gossip about others.

8. You keep things confidential.

9. You show up on time.

10. You lead by example.

SELF-REFLECTION TIME

- In your words, describe what it means to be a "leader of integrity."

- Why do you think integrity is such an important trait for a leader?

"Make your 'yes' mean yes and your 'no' mean no."

– John Wooden

.

CHAPTER 3

Lead with Influence

Throughout life people come and go, and some of them influence how we think and act. They may not have been life altering, but they influenced us at the time.

Effective leadership is about influence. Note: The first person you must influence and inspire is yourself. Then you can influence those who know and respect you. They may be people you have established a personal relationship with or they may be people who don't know you but believe in your integrity. Either way, if you want to achieve your goals, people must have enough faith in you that they are willing to be influenced by you.

Make no mistake—the influence we are talking about here is not authoritarian. Forcing people is not influencing them. Bullying does not mean influencing. Those who use these tactics are looking only for compliance. They have a "Do what I say" approach, and their autocratic style of leadership usually leads to a toxic culture. Such people criticize, blame, don't listen well, defend their egos, and demand. They just like to boss others around—not exactly influential, is it?

Influence is not about forcing but rather about getting others to follow you because they want to. Great leaders know that getting to this point is through the nurturing of relationships. Over time, these relationships become stronger and rise to a higher level of trust. The higher the level of trust you have, the more influence you have. It is important to remember that as a leader, the more influence you have, the greater is your responsibility to use it for the betterment of others.

Leaders who are influential are open-minded, encourage others, demonstrate empathy, create the vision and lead by example. That's why they're influential; they've earned it.

George Raveling, former head basketball coach at Washington State University, the University of Iowa, and the University of Southern California, influenced many people—his young athletes, his staff, his fans, and many others. He takes a broad view of influence: "In an increasingly collaborative and connected world, achievement depends more than ever on the subtle art of influence. Often, we can spend far too much time looking out for ourselves. If we want to stand out from the crowd, help someone. To build stronger connections with people, we need to influence our organizations, teams, and communities to look for common ground and opportunities to share with each other's expertise."

Another person whose influence brought about huge transformation was Nelson Mandela. The enormity of his influence on the world was and still is undeniable. He fought for years against apartheid in South Africa, enduring a long imprisonment and a constant stream of indignities en route to dismantling the South African National Party's legally codified racism. He became the first black president of South Africa and won the Nobel Peace Prize. He did not accomplish any of this by being coercive or corrosive.

Another fine example of earning influence is England and Liverpool football captain, Jordan Henderson. Back in 2012, Jordan was almost sold to a different club as he wasn't deemed "good enough." Many even criticized that he was there in the first place. However, Henderson decided to stay put at Liverpool and prove his worth. Fast forward to 2020. The highly respected and influential Henderson—now captain of the club—lifted the Champions league trophy and the 2019/2020 Premier league trophy. When asked how he'd won the respect of his fellow teammates, the coach and the fans, he replied, "I try to lead the team by example. For me as a captain and leader, I believe that you can't influence your teammates if you don't first have their trust and respect."

Like Henderson, leaders who have influence are trustworthy and genuine. Their behaviors and actions back up their words. The people they lead are drawn to them by their authenticity and charisma. They establish shared vision and values for their people, inspire commitment by engaging every team member, and strategically and collaboratively direct initiatives in order to achieve that shared vision.

Those who apply influence rather than asserting authority are the likeliest to succeed, especially in the long run. The bottom line is that team members will follow leaders they trust and believe in—ones who demonstrate values and behaviors they align with. People want to work with someone who has the individual's and team's best interests at heart: It is evidence of the leader's fundamental integrity.

Earning influence instead of wielding authority is one of the practices a good leader with higher aspirations should adopt.

Moreover, being influential is not about what we learn *to do to* others but what we learn *to be for* others. It's about consistently being the kind of leader team members want to follow.

SELF-REFLECTION TIME

- ◎ As a leader, what ways do you feel you could enhance your influence on those you lead?

- ◎ Think of a leader who has influenced you in some way. What was it about them that left such an impression on you?

"What counts in life is not the mere fact that we have lived; it is the difference we have made in the lives of others that will determine the significance of the life we lead."

– Nelson Mandela

CHAPTER 4

Lead with High Standards

In my 25+ years of being in the performance and leadership fields, I have never witnessed a successful organization or winning team where the standards were average. Consistency in high standards leads to excellence. Great leaders just don't allow mediocrity.

One of the most successful women's college basketball programs ever is at the University of Connecticut (UConn). Since their coach, Geno Auriemma, took over in 1985, UConn has broken multiple records, including two of the longest winning streaks in NCAA Division One women's college basketball history: 111 straight wins and 91 straight wins.

In collegiate athletics, no one demands a higher standard than Auriemma. When asked the key to such sustained success, he credits two factors. The first is accountability—his players hold themselves and each other accountable on a daily basis. The second is setting and maintaining high standards, starting with how he sets standards for himself.

Indeed, as a leader, you set the example by focusing on your own accountability for maintaining high standards. You can have your values plastered all over the walls, but the most powerful way to display them will always be through your own behaviors and actions. This is how you build your reputation and identity. This is how you build the best people and how you achieve the best results.

In a tweet sent out by Adam Grant, author of several best-selling books such as *Think Again* and *Give and Take*, he cites a clear-cut opinion about standards, accountability and leadership: "Weak leaders hold their teams accountable for their own bad decisions. They blame others in order to hide their errors in judgment. Strong leaders ask their teams to hold them accountable for making good decisions. They rely on others to help them prevent their errors in judgment."

Another great example of maintaining high standards is former Manchester United manager and coach, Sir Alex Ferguson. Anyone who knows the English Premier League will tell you how quickly a player can be sacked from his position if he starts to demand less than the best of himself. Ferguson was at the club for an astonishing 26 years and won 13 league titles along with 25 other domestic and international trophies. A huge part of his success came down to the high standards to which he held every member of the club; no one was given a pass. Ferguson believed that everything done at the club was about maintaining high standards.

Sir Alex set the example. He was the first to arrive and the last to leave. He didn't tolerate behaviors that would in any way jeopardize the club's culture. Without a doubt, the successes of Manchester United during his career there came down to the standards he set, lived and maintained.

Benfica, the most popular football club in Portuguese history, is another team with high standards. I visited them toward the end of 2021, and it was easy to see why they have achieved sustained success. Starting from my first conversation with the staff, it was obvious that there was a standard of excellence in place. They interacted positively and comfortably with one another. Even the younger academy kids there greeted others with a smile as they passed in the hallway. It is one of the many revealing details that reflected the culture of excellence present and the values board hanging prominently on the wall for all to see.

One sad fact I've learned over the years of working with teams and organizations is that excellence isn't for everyone. When driving high standards and aiming for excellence in your organization, understand that not everyone will aspire to meet expectations. Not everyone will agree to them or have the discipline to carry them out. That's why some people will never be the right fit for your organization or team. You'll find that some people possess the right qualifications or skills but lack the discipline, work ethic and commitment. They reflect badly on you and on everyone else. Moreover, they can undermine everything. Do not tolerate laziness and low standards.

The truth is that no culture of excellence was ever achieved unless high standards were owned by its leaders and team members on a daily basis.

4 Reasons Why Leading with High Standards Is Important

1. They create a culture of accountability
2. They provide clarity about what is acceptable and what isn't
3. They provide identity
4. They drive the behaviors that lead to top-notch outcomes

SELF-REFLECTION TIME

- ◎ As a leader, list some of the standards you have within your organization. Will they lead to a culture of excellence?

- ◎ What standards do you feel need to be improved or introduced within your organization right now?

"Once you bid farewell to high standards and discipline, you say goodbye to success."

– Sir Alex Ferguson

CHAPTER 5

Lead with Self-Awareness

I recently saw a presentation by Steve Hansen, the World Cup winning rugby coach of the All Blacks (New Zealand). He emphasized the importance of self-awareness for coaches and leaders. "Knowing yourself," he said, "is the most important thing."

He further explained the importance of taking deliberate action in growing yourself every day. Each one of us has shortcomings we need to work on, not just as coaches or leaders but, more importantly, as human beings. He acknowledged that he had had to work on becoming a better communicator, specifically a better listener, as he had always liked to be the one talking.

I've been asked what exactly self-awareness is. It's the ability to be conscious of, acknowledge and understand our own behaviors, values, perspectives, strengths and weaknesses.

Being more self-aware and seeing ourselves more honestly helps us become more confident and tolerant. We are able to build stronger relationships, make sounder decisions and communicate more effectively. As Hansen said, when we become more self-aware, we become more in touch not only with ourselves but also with others—crucial for the person in charge. Leaders with self-awareness understand and manage their personal strengths and weaknesses to optimize leadership impact. They know what they're doing as they do it, read situations well and can make necessary adjustments in the moment.

When we aren't honest with ourselves, we lose sight of who we really are. We may overlook problems of our own that we criticize in others. To paraphrase the famous Robert Burns quote, "I wish someone could give us the power to see ourselves as others see us." We may think or hope we know how others see us, but how they actually see us may come as a surprise.

Developing self-awareness is a crucial first step in effective leadership because it lays the foundation upon which emotional and social intelligence and empathy are built. Emotional self-awareness helps leaders link their emotions to the effectiveness of their interactions with others. A great believer in this concept, Daniel Goleman, author of *Emotional Intelligence*, identifies self-awareness as the cornerstone to emotional intelligence, which he defines as the ability to monitor our emotions and thoughts from moment to moment. It is fundamental to understanding ourselves better.

A few years back when I really dedicated myself to becoming more self-aware, I discovered many flaws and shortcomings that I wasn't even aware of. It wasn't a pleasant experience, to be honest, but a very worthwhile one. As I shared in my book *Developing a Winning Attitude and Mindset*, each evening I reflect on the day I've had. I ask myself 3 simple questions:

1. What did I do well today?
2. What could I have done better today?
3. Who did I make better today?

These 3 questions, which can make someone a better human being, are just as effective in making someone a better leader. Taking just a few minutes to think about and then answer these questions has certainly helped me become both a better person and a better leader. My relationships are more meaningful because I have more understanding, patience and compassion for others.

Implementing this practice can allow you to understand what others are thinking, what they're feeling, how they perceive you—

and your attitude and your responses to them—in the moment. It is a state of heightened overall awareness. Furthermore, having good and accurate self-awareness helps leaders be more comfortable in their own skin.

As with any leadership skill, self-awareness can and should be practiced. A simple way to start is by answering the 3 questions. You will begin to see yourself with clearer eyes and be able to adjust your leadership strategy accordingly.

SELF-REFLECTION TIME

- ◎ For a leader, what are some of the benefits of practicing self-reflection?
- ◎ Name something you did well and something you could have done better today.

"We cannot change what we are not aware of, and once we are aware, we cannot help but change."

– Sheryl Sandberg

CHAPTER 6

Lead with Example

In 2019, I was invited to be the keynote speaker at the Badminton World Federation (BWF) coaches conference in Basel, Switzerland. Among the impressive line-up of speakers was the Chef De Mission of Paralympics GB, Penny Briscoe OBE (a high honor in Great Britain).

An amazing woman with an abundant amount of energy and zest for life, Penny spoke about her experiences managing the Great Britain Paralympics team and especially her time at the 2016 Rio Paralympic Games. What really caught my attention among the slides in her presentation was a picture of her mopping the floor in an apartment in the athletes' village.

I was intrigued by this photo and after her presentation, I tracked her down in the hallway. I wanted to find out what that was all about. She said that when they had arrived at the Paralympic village, there was a number of issues that needed quick resolution. Cleaning had been suspended at the end of the Olympics due to security concerns and there was limited time to get the accommodation ready for the team (over 450 athletes and staff). Instead of waiting for assistance, Penny took it upon herself to find a mop and bucket and started mopping the floors.

Needless to say, this was incredibly inspiring. The most important person on the team was doing work that was far from her job description. What a great example of humility in a leader. Penny was not afraid to get her hands dirty.

People are influenced by the example of our behaviors. While our words matter, our actions matter far more. Leaders must first be what they want to see: Set the example that inspires trust. When leaders are role models, successfully accomplishing goals and conducting day-to-day tasks, the team follows. Justin Langer, head coach of the Australian Cricket Team, is passionate about this subject. "If you preach excellence, but practice mediocrity, you're nothing but a liar." If you want to gain the confidence and trust of your team, you must set the benchmark.

When working with teams, one commonality I've discovered in the very best ones is that they always have one or more players who are experienced leaders and who are also considered to have the highest work ethic. One example is the England Lionesses football captain, Steph Houghton, who I interviewed on my podcast. Steph said she wouldn't ask a team player to do something she wasn't willing to do herself. Leaders like Steph walk their talk, and their teammates see them doing it every day.

Awhile back, when I was working for a national tennis federation in Europe, I attended a team meeting where a coach was speaking to a group of young players about the importance of living the lifestyle of a champion. He emphasized the necessity of getting the right amount of sleep, preparing and eating healthy foods—all very good points.

His speech was great; however, it fell on deaf ears because the coach himself was not living by those standards. He was indeed setting several examples for his young players, but none of them were good. His habits didn't portray the expectations he set for his team. His eating habits were poor, and he sometimes had take-out fast-food on his office desk and a soda in his hand.

While he was talking, I looked around and saw how unengaged the kids were. When they were dismissed, I could hear them snickering about what the coach had just said. Fortunately, it was clear that his example wasn't one that would be followed anytime soon. The coach wasn't walking his talk: He had forfeited his credibility.

Early in 2020, I was visiting the Scottish football club Glasgow Rangers training facility in Milngavie. I got to spend the day presenting to some of the coaches and performance staff there. What impressed me most was the example of their manager, the former Liverpool and England captain Steven Gerrard. I saw that he made it a point to interact with all the players, coaches and staff. He demonstrated the importance of masterfully adapting his approach to each team member.

Later I had lunch with head coach Michael Beale, head of performance Jordan Milsom and Steven. It was then that I discovered just how humble, interesting and engaging Steven was. He made me feel valued and included. And around 6:00 that evening, when most of the staff and players had left the facility, I strolled past the gym only to see Steven himself in there training alone. And when I left the facility around 7:00, Steven was still there.

Leading by example creates a picture of what's possible. Steven was and certainly is an example of just that. He is the kind of leader who won't ask anything of his players that he's not willing to do himself. Steven sets the bar high for standards and practicing what you preach high.

Steven's former teammate at Liverpool, Xavi Alonso, believes that Steven always showed his fellow players how to be their best selves. "As a player, he was inspirational to all the players around him, a proper leader who always led by example. That transition from a captain into management has come very naturally for him."

A great example of on-the-field leadership occurred during the 2020 Euro Football Championships. Just minutes before halftime in one of the opening matches between Denmark and Finland, Denmark's star player, Christian Eriksen collapsed on the field. Most everyone stopped in their tracks, but team captain Simon Kjaer rushed forward to roll Eriksen onto his side, stabilize his head and open his mouth to prevent him from choking on his tongue. He administered CPR until, just seconds later, the medical staff arrived to continue the procedure on the 29-year-old who had suffered a cardiac arrest. Kjaer then organized his teammates in a semi-circle to shield Eriksen from the view of the public and television cameras. As Eriksen's distraught wife, Sabrina Kvist Jensen, came running onto the field fearing the worst, it was again Kjaer, along with goalkeeper Kasper Schmeichel, who hugged and reassured her. Kjaer stepped up and took the action that probably saved Eriksen's life. He led by example.

When you lead by example, your actions influence others to behave and respond in ways that are valuable for the culture of your organization. If you want your influence to be positive and impactful, be clear about what you want from others, and then make sure your actions support that vision. When you do this, you are leading in an intentional and productive way. As author and leadership expert John C. Maxwell says, "A leader is one who knows the way, goes the way, and shows the way."

5 Ways to Lead by Example

1. Demonstrate character and loyalty.
2. Be responsible and credible.
3. Be honest.
4. Be courageous.
5. Show vulnerability.

SELF-REFLECTION TIME

- As a leader, how do you walk the talk and be a good example to those you lead?
- In what ways can you improve the example you set?

As a player, he [Steven Gerrard], was inspirational to all the players around him, a proper leader who always led by example. That transition from captain into management has come very naturally for him."

– Xavi Alonso

CHAPTER 7

Lead with Trust

Trust is basic to effective leadership. Without it, leaders don't have faith in their people, and their people don't have faith in their leaders. Trust is the glue that holds everyone and everything together. As Brazilian educator and philosopher Paulo Freire said, "The trust of the people in the leaders reflects the confidence of the leaders in the people." Each empowers the other.

In 2016, after a record 108-year baseball World Series drought, the Chicago Cubs won in the seventh and final game. Their inspirational coach Joe Maddon explained his managerial philosophy in an interview afterward. "Before you can manage and lead, you must establish trust. And before you can establish trust, you need to establish a personal relationship with your players."

This is a philosophy I use when consulting with corporate or sports teams. I impress upon the leaders that before people can buy into the vision, they first need to buy into the person the leader is. They want to know they can trust the person because people don't trust a title or a position. They trust a human being.

David Horsager, author of the book *The Trust Edge: How Top Leaders Gain Faster Results, Deeper Relationships, and a Stronger Bottom Line*, puts it this way: "You can have a compelling vision, rock solid strategy, excellent communication skills, innovative insight and a skilled team, but if people don't trust you, you will never get the results you want."

So how do leaders build trust? One way is to be the example. Do their actions and behaviors match their words? Do they walk the talk? Leaders who *earn* trust are respected and valued by their people. They live life with integrity.

Former England Lionesses football captain and coach of Manchester United women's team, Casey Stoney agrees. She shared with me the importance of building trust with her players and the staff. Casey believes that one of the key foundations to building trust is having the tough and honest conversations. She said that even though it is at times uncomfortable and she doesn't necessarily enjoy them, they have to take place.

Justin Langer, "JL," the Australian cricket coach and former international cricketer, found himself coaching under stressful circumstances and expressed a view of trust similar to Stoney's. He was appointed to the head role in May 2018, following a ball tampering scandal under the previous head coach. Australian cricket was at its lowest. In an interview on leadership, JL addressed the subject of trust. "One thing I've learned in leadership is that trust is everything. If you have the courage to have honest conversations, you build trust. And with more trust, you can build more honest conversations." And so it grows.

Trust in leadership can be lost even before it is established. It can happen when a leader's actions and behaviors don't match their words. It can happen when there is inconsistency in the values and the standards. And it can happen when there is micromanagement. Leaders who are always looking over their team members' shoulders relay the message "I don't trust you and that's why I'm watching you."

Great leaders instead show trust in their team to carry out the appointed tasks. They are there for guidance and support, but they give their team the responsibility that creates ownership.

Trust can be lost when relationships aren't properly nurtured. A leader needs to be transparent. Leaders who show only their perfections or their highlights reel will not be trusted. No one expects the perfect model, only a consistently honest and authentic one. You build trust as your people learn that you, too, are human, and you, too, make mistakes, and especially, you, too, are willing to admit it.

So, how can you build and lead with TRUST?

Here are 5 factors basic to building TRUST:

Time: Trust cannot be fast tracked. It takes time. Just as in a romantic relationship, trust is built by consistency in behaviors, actions and commitment.

Relationships: When you show genuine interest in others, solid relationships are formed. Building meaningful relationships is about making a deeper connection and showing that you care about your people.

Understanding: Trust also comes from having empathy, appreciation and a good understanding of others. It involves seeing things from another person's perspective and being open to listening to them.

Sharing Accolades: A leader who takes all the glory for the successes and blames others for failures will not be trusted or respected. A leader who shares or deflects successes to their team earns trust and admiration. It's about the "we" and not the "me."

Truthfulness: Great leaders might not be liked all the time, but they are respected because they tell the truth. Being consistently candid and nurturing a culture of openness and honesty builds commitment, collaboration and trust. General Electric Chairman and CEO Jack Welch noted, "Trust happens when leaders are transparent. Being truthful takes courage as it involves the hard conversations and making the tough decisions."

Trust is an essential element in leadership and in team productivity. Without it, you're unlikely to get anything meaningful done. But with it, teams and organizations can accomplish everything they set out to do and more. If trust between and among you and your team members isn't strong, work on it. Set the example. Show your team members how vital trust is to you by demonstrating your trust in them.

SELF-REFLECTION TIME

- ⦿ Think back to a leader in your life that you perhaps didn't completely trust. What were some of the characteristics that made you feel that way?

- ⦿ What are some of the ways you build trust with those you lead? What other actions can you take?

"Before we can manage and lead, you must establish trust. And before you can establish trust, you need to establish a personal relationship with your players."

– Joe Maddon

CHAPTER 8

Lead with Vision

D id you know that Thomas Edison failed 10,000 times before successfully inventing the light bulb? Furthermore, Walt Disney was fired from a newspaper because he "lacked imagination and had no good ideas." Oprah Winfrey was fired from her job as a television reporter because she was "unfit for TV." Steven Spielberg received film school rejections three times. Michael Jordan was cut from his high school basketball team. What was it that led these talented and successful people to continue despite multiple failures and rejections? It was that they all had a deep inner belief in a vision for their future.

Vision is priceless. It is the big picture of where you want to go and how you plan to get there. Great leaders have a clear and optimistic vision and see positive outcomes. They wholeheartedly believe that they can make a difference in the world.

Michael Hyatt, author, speaker, CEO and founder of Michael Hyatt & Company, has written several books about leadership, productivity, and goal setting. He believes strongly that vision is the foundation of everything. "Vision is the prerequisite for leadership. If you don't have clarity around the destination, you really can't lead your people to a better future. I think that's the number one job, to set the vision."

Indeed, the vision the leader has created is one of the chief factors in an organization's success. However, it is not just about creating the vision, but also about having clarity of the vision. Over the years I have been called on to advise many organizations, teams and companies where the employees or team members didn't have clarity about the vision, and things were falling apart. Whose fault was that? It was the mistake of the leader who did not effectively communicate that long-term goal well enough.

Sharing a vision is similar to laying out a road map that identifies the end point and the route you need to take to get there. If you don't share the vision with your team members, it's like putting them on a driverless bus and hoping they arrive at the destination you have in mind. It's little wonder then that people lose the commitment, motivation and desire needed to reach intended goals.

Not communicating your vision is a common mistake that many leaders make: you cannot overcommunicate the vision. In fact, successfully conveying this message is one of the benchmarks of leaders in successful organizations and team cultures. How is this accomplished? Great leaders repeat their message as often as possible; for example, through reminders in meetings, conversations and general emails. The vision is broadcast as much as possible, in every way possible. The Reverend Theodore Hesburgh, president of the University of Notre Dame 1952-87, noted, "The very essence of leadership is that you have a vision. It's got to be a vision you articulate clearly and forcefully on every occasion." Laying out your vision sets both organizational direction and purpose for your team. It generates belief, commitment and enthusiasm.

Most often, when a new coach or leader takes over a team or in an organization, they talk about their vision. They communicate their vision of the people they want, the culture they want and how they want things to operate on a daily basis. It's important for the coach or leader to fully communicate this information to those who will play roles in implementation.

The vision of the leader attracts and affects every team member engaged in living the set of actions, beliefs, values, and goals of the organization. They feel part of a greater purpose and share the leader's vision and passion.

Business leader and former CEO of General Electric Jack Welch said, "Good leaders create a vision, articulate the vision, passionately own the vision, and relentlessly drive it to completion." A vision is much more than a destination. It's thought, emotion and action. Great leaders can see into the future, and it is one of the qualities that separate the average ones from the great ones.

Over the years, the leaders I've observed who have been extraordinarily successful have had their vision in place. They led with purpose and provided inspiration. Moreover, they made others feel appreciated, provided opportunities for them to grow both professionally and personally and let the enthusiasm they nurtured carry them to success.

SELF-REFLECTION TIME

- How clear are you about your vision and the various actions you have to take to achieve it?

- As a leader, how clear have you been in delivering your vision to your people? Have you asked them?

"The very essence of leadership is that you have a vision. It's got to be a vision you articulate clearly and forcefully on every occasion."

– Reverend Theodore Hesburgh

CHAPTER 9

Lead with Curiosity

Walt Whitman said, "Be curious, not judgmental." Indeed, the most effective leaders enjoy the benefits of curiosity and an open-mindedness. At the risk of stating the obvious, curious people learn interesting information that enhances their ability to lead in a variety of ways. Bonus: It also makes them more interesting. Curious leaders are receptive to new ideas rather than blindly clinging to their current knowledge and beliefs. They know that dogmatism is the enemy of growth.

Great leaders challenge the status quo. The mindset of "well, that's how things have always been done around here" has no place in their organization.

One morning a while ago, I had breakfast in Manhattan Beach, California, with a good friend who heads a sports management agency. I showed him an article and asked for his opinion. He replied, "You shouldn't read everything you believe or believe everything you read." It's so easy to seek out the things and people we agree with (and who agree with us) to validate ourselves. In a way, when we look only for validation for what we believe, we are simply stroking fragile egos and insecurities. Exploring places we have not intellectually been before keeps our thought processes stimulated and fresh.

We experience the world through a filter of our values, beliefs, ideas and emotions. There is a wonderful domino effect for curious and open-minded leaders. It starts with the fact that they are less judgmental and respect other people's opinions, choices and beliefs.

They might not always agree, but they are open to hear what others have to say. Consequently, they tend to be more likable and get along with others. People tend to feel more open with them and freer to share their ideas, opinions and viewpoints without the fear of being judged. This openness nurtures new concepts and heightened performances.

The fact is that even when you are a leader, you will not have all the solutions for all the problems. Leading with a growth mentality and open-minded approach can provide crucial and interesting facts in clutch situations. Furthermore, it can spark just the creativity you need to find a solution when facing the unknown.

In my journey, first as a coach and now as a consultant in leadership and mindset, I have always believed in the power of 4 simple words when working with an athlete or client: "What do you think?" When I ask this question, not only does it open me up to what they are thinking and feeling, but more importantly it makes them part of the decision making process. In fact, hearing their opinions and viewpoints can influence my own.

By and large, great leaders are deeply interested in listening to others. They listen more than they talk. They are what I term 80/20 communicators; they listen 80 percent of the time and talk 20 percent of the time. They know that listening gives them the opportunity to explore someone else's body of knowledge. You can, too—you can learn from just about anyone, regardless of age, status or level of experience.

Interest in new ideas from outside their specialty fields sets great leaders apart from their less inquisitive colleagues. Eddie Jones, the England Rugby Coach, is one such leader who is always curious and looks to other sports, like hockey, cricket and football, for new ideas. Pep Guardiola, the Barcelona and Manchester City title winning soccer coach, holds in high esteem Julio Velasco, the Argentinian professional volleyball coach and athletic administrator. It's believed that Pep even travelled hundreds of miles just so he could meet Velasco in person and learn from him.

Another inquiring mind is Steve Kerr, the former NBA Basketball player and a multiple NBA winning coach with the Golden State Warriors. He, too, has a deep interest in learning from other sports. In fact, Kerr admits to reading and rereading Timothy Gallwey's *The Inner Game of Tennis*, which explores the mindset of a very different sport. Only a curious and open mind allows itself to find transferrable ideas from one to the other.

The Eddie Joneses, Pep Guardiolas and Steve Kerrs of the world are constantly looking for practices and methods that can improve their own sport. When they find concepts with potential, they explore them enthusiastically.

Curious leaders are forward thinking. They want tomorrow to be an improvement over today. In that pursuit, every day offers opportunities to learn something new and to try something different. Enjoy the benefits of a receptive mindset. Become an even better leader by staying more and more curious.

SELF-REFLECTION TIME

- Would you describe yourself as a curious leader? What do you do that demonstrates this?

- Outside of your chosen field, what other fields, industries, etc. are you learning and expanding your knowledge from?

"We keep moving forward, opening new doors, and doing new things, because we're curious, and curiosity keeps leading us down new paths."

– Walt Disney

CHAPTER 10

Lead with Care

Franklin D. Roosevelt famously said, "People don't care how much you know until they know how much you care." Thinking back to your younger years, was this true for you? From my youth, I vividly remember the people in leadership positions who showed they really cared about me. They were the ones who most influenced my behavior, my beliefs and the rest of my life. I like to think that one of their principal goals was to make an impact and leave their legacy by positively influencing the lives of the people they led.

People may admire how good you are in your field, but they will *never forget* how much you cared about them. When people feel your interest in them, you have begun building the foundations of trust-based relationships.

Let's look at the Disney Institute based in Orlando. Disney prides itself on its culture and puts care at the top of its list of core values. Disney decision makers believe that the more they show they genuinely care about their employees, the more their employees will care about their customers and about one another, and the better their employees will facilitate, support and personalize the guest experience. The domino effect at its best.

When I ask people about the leaders, coaches, teachers, managers, etc. they liked and respected the most, they nearly always mention those who took time just for them. I recently consulted at a well-known university here in the United States where the head coach of the tennis team was struggling to connect with his players.

The coach, who was in his mid 50s, had a wealth of experience and knowledge. However, on observing some of his interactions with the players, I could see an obvious void in the player-coach relationship.

The coach's attention focused on the game and results with almost no personal interaction or social talk. And therein lay the problem. Even though on paper he was a coach with what it takes to build a bonded, collaborative team, he fostered no close relationships on any level.

In my one-on-one meetings with the players later that afternoon, their feedback was that even though they had a lot of respect for him as a coach, they felt he cared about them only as players. He was all about their game and not about them.

When I brought this message to the coach, he was quite taken aback by the news. In his mind, he had great connections with his team. But after I challenged him with a few questions about his players, he realized that he actually didn't know them well enough in a personal way. He admitted that he hadn't taken the time or made the effort to get to know them well at all.

In his landmark book *How to Win Friends and Influence People*, Dale Carnegie wrote, "You can make more friends in two months by showing interest in others than you can in two years by trying to get others interested in you." I relayed this philosophy to the coach and, fortunately, he took it to heart. He decided to direct energy to getting to know his players better as people. Fast forward a few months: The team's culture improved and their results soared—thanks to a seasoned coach who was willing to listen to his players and work on relationships with and among them.

Without a doubt, the best coaches and leaders whose teams I've been privileged to be on had one thing in common—they all genuinely cared about me. Interactions with them always made me feel safe. Whoever they spent time with felt like the most important person in the world. Leadership was never about them, but about those standing in front of them.

A few years ago, when I lived in Sarasota, Florida, well known author John Maxwell was preaching at my church. John spoke about being a caring leader. "Caring is about giving your time to others, sitting down and listening to them, valuing them, and respecting them." Leaders who care for their people make time for them and listen to them intentionally.

Great leaders treat those they lead as equals rather than as people who are beneath them. As Simon Sinek, author of the book *Leaders Eat Last*, wrote, "Leadership is not a rank; it is a responsibility. Leadership is not about being in charge; it is about taking care of those in your charge. And when we take care of our people, our people will take care of us." In organizations that implement this strategy, not only do team members not want to leave, but other prospects will want to join there.

Great leaders go beyond caring only about their people's work skills and performances. They are genuinely interested in them as human beings who have lives outside of the workplace. They ask questions about their spouses, partners, kids, etc. They learn about their hobbies and outside activities. They set time aside to create those winning moments that may seem like simple get-to-know-you stuff but are actually the ones who tell their team members that they are important.

Showing interest puts the focus on someone else. Think about a coach or a leader who made a positive indelible impact on your life by caring enough to pay attention to you. Be that person to others.

SELF-REFLECTION TIME

- ◉ As a leader, how do you show those you lead that you truly care?

- ◉ Think about someone who has made a constructive impact on your life. What was it about this person that still resonates with you? What can you do to have that kind of influence on others?

"A winning culture is where acts of care are shown on a daily basis. Care is what connects people."

– Steve Cooke

CHAPTER 11

Lead with Authenticity

A few years ago, I surveyed a group of working professionals that included managers, coaches, teachers and people from the corporate and sales worlds. Out of a list of 10 leadership qualities that leaders could have (for example, humility, experience, knowledge, etc.), I asked them to list their top three. It can be no surprise that authenticity placed at the very top of the list of the majority.

Merriam-Webster's defines authenticity as "being true to one's own personality, spirit or character." You are seeing authenticity when you see someone walking their talk.

What less-than-transparent leaders fail to realize is that people don't want to follow someone who is not authentic or honest. They don't want a leader who is pretending to be someone they are not or someone who tries to portray the perfect image. What they do want is someone they can relate to, trust and confide in: someone who is not afraid to be open and at times show some vulnerability.

Best-selling author and speaker Brené Brown writes, "To be authentic, we must cultivate the courage to be imperfect—and vulnerable. We have to believe that we are fundamentally worthy of love and acceptance, just as we are. I've learned that there is no better way to invite more grace, gratitude and joy into our lives than by mindfully practicing authenticity."

One such example is the incredibly charismatic and popular coach of Liverpool Football Club, Jurgen Klopp. After joining the English club in 2015 from the German club Borussia Dortmund,

Klopp steadily built a cult-like following at the Merseyside club in England.

Having achieved success in prestigious competitions such as the Champions League, World Club Championship and the Premier League, Klopp jokingly referred to himself as the "normal one"—a comment he made after Jose Mourinho, manager of rival club Chelsea, referred to himself as "the special one." Klopp knew the value of being relatable and authentic.

When Klopp's players were asked in an interview what they felt made Klopp so well liked, the word "authenticity" came up. Club captain Jordan Henderson noted that the likable German coach consistently "models the habits, attitudes, and actions he wants from his players and staff. He also isn't afraid to be vulnerable and display his emotions." Klopp has built a culture where chemistry and authenticity are unmistakable. Former club legend Robbie Fowler added that "Jurgen is as real as they come. The person you see on TV is the same person away from it. I think that's why people love him so much."

Genuine leaders demonstrate self-awareness. They take time up front to reflect upon their actions, behaviors and decisions. They lead with their heart and with the courage and empathy that come only from listening to the heart.

Fortunately, when a leader is able to practice empathy and humility, trust is earned and authenticity is established within the team. Authentic and trusted leaders have the humility to seek team members' opinions and build a culture that prioritizes a humble pursuit of the truth.

As with Jurgen Klopp, genuine leaders' words match their actions. They promote an open and honest culture. The image they project in public is not much different from how they really are in private. They don't hide their failures and weaknesses; they have the courage to own up to them. And when they are wrong, they are not afraid to admit it and apologize.

In addition, they share successes with their team. They publicly give credit where it is due and openly share the spotlight and achievements with everyone. Authentic leaders love to see others succeed. This is something that sets an authentic leader apart from other leaders. Selfish leaders bask in the glory when success comes around and place blame on others when things go wrong. It's a good bet that they don't realize that their efforts to make themselves look good have quite the opposite effect.

Like Klopp, authentic leaders add value to people, both professionally and personally. As a result, others follow them. Isn't that what you want?

SELF-REFLECTION TIME

- ◉ As a leader, why do you think authenticity is so important in leadership?

- ◉ Do you sometimes find it difficult to be vulnerable with those you lead? If you answered yes, why is that? How can you address it?

"Authenticity means erasing the gap between what you firmly believe inside and what you reveal to the outside world."

– Adam Grant

CHAPTER 12

Lead with Calmness

A ah, calmness—the ability to keep your wits about you when the world around you is crumbling.

Back in 2020, threats of shortages in some products—perhaps most famously pasta, toilet paper and disinfecting products—may have become self-fulfilling scarcities. Indeed, some of those empty shelves may not have been so starkly visible without shopper frenzy. Frenzy, when everyone would have benefitted from calmness.

When we most needed cool heads, both among leaders and among the general population, uproar at the grocery store made it hard to enjoy spaghetti, let alone stay clean. And there are times of even greater adversity when maintaining composure may come in handy.

Case in point: the miracle on the Hudson. On January 15, 2009, Capt. Chesley "Sully" Sullenberger's US Airways Airbus A320 hit a flock of geese shortly after takeoff from New York's LaGuardia Airport en route to Charlotte, North Carolina. The strike caused both engines to lose power some 2,800 feet up. Sully had less than 3 minutes to land the airplane. In dramatic fashion, he put it down safely on the surface of the Hudson River, saving all 155 passengers and crew. In fact, the 2016 film *Sully: Miracle on the Hudson*, starring Tom Hanks and directed by Clint Eastwood, told the story. Because of his incredible aeronautical skills and ability to remain calm, Sully was able to make a clear-headed decision. Calmness at its best.

In uncertain times, your people are looking to you, the leader, to remain calm under pressure and provide direction and stability. How is this achieved? One way is to communicate consistently and steadily through good times and bad.

The ability to calm agitation fosters collaboration and builds trust. It nurtures the belief that however bad things seem to be, the reliable leader has everyone's backs. They can keep the faith, pull together and master the challenges.

I love to watch reruns of the hilarious American comedy series *The Office*, which stars Steve Carrell. In a scene called "The Fire Drill," the boss, Michael Scott (played by Carrell), frantically runs out of his office screaming that everyone should just remain calm and not panic. He might be saying the right things, but how he's delivering them and how he's behaving not only cause everyone in the office to completely freak out, but also cause utter confusion. It's a clear example of "Do as I say and not as I do."

So, what about you? What kind of leader are you in times of crisis, uncertainty or chaos? We might not all have the self-control or in-the-moment decision making skills of Captain Sully, but do the people you lead at least feel that you bring a sense of security, direction and calmness? Do your people feel that you are competent and reliable in times of adversity?

Tony Smith, the Australian rugby coach who has coached England, Great Britain and the Warrington Wolves to success, has remained calm under pressure countless times. "The best answers," he said, "are when you're calm. Calm and rational." During a crisis, or even the perception of a crisis, your people require the best of your direction and leadership. As the leader goes, so goes the team. They don't expect you to have all the answers, but they do expect you to have a stable plan. When the going gets tough, the team expects, and needs, you to set the example, to keep calm and carry on.

SELF-REFLECTION TIME

- ⦿ As a leader, when adversity strikes, how calm and in control are you? What would your people say?

- ⦿ How good would you say you are in communicating calmness and composure to your people in times of adversity? What would your people say?

"The best answers are when you're calm. Calm and rational. When the going gets tough, the team expects, and needs you to set the example, to keep calm and carry on."

– Tony Smith

CHAPTER 13

Lead with Belief

Becoming a great leader requires 3 strong beliefs:

1. Belief in yourself
2. Belief in your vision
3. Belief in your people

Belief in Yourself

If you don't first believe in yourself, why should others? Your people want to know that you have the strength and self-confidence to lead them through both good times and bad. These are qualities that inspire your people to follow, respect and support you. They will see what you are trying to achieve and will want to share in that success as part of your team.

Everybody encounters blips along the way. Belief in yourself can wane from time to time. Much like an athlete who can lose their self-belief, so, too, can a leader. Remember that that doesn't mean you have lost your competence or abilities as a leader. You're only human, so from time to time you will make mistakes—wrong choices or wrong decisions. It happens to everyone, even those with many years' experience. It's important to accept those days, reflect on what went wrong, then get up the next day determined to get back on track.

Just because they exude confidence and belief, that doesn't mean great leaders think they have all the answers. They remain open to learning and growing. Their confidence is revealed by the people they surround themselves with—people who are more competent in certain areas than they are. They believe in themselves and in their team to achieve success.

Peter Goodyer is the CEO and headmaster at Bede's School, an independent, co-educational school in East Sussex, England. On a speaking visit to the school, I was able to ask Peter over lunch about the importance of self-belief in a leader. He said, "There is no doubt that confidence and belief in oneself are necessities in leadership. To have a strength of conviction is vital when making complex decisions and seeking solutions to complex problems. However, it is also crucial that as a leader you have humility, that you are willing to accept when you need the input of others and that, importantly, we very much rely on the expertise of others to assist us in reaching our decisions and conclusions. A leader who has self-belief to me is someone who is comfortable being themselves, they know what they know and are willing to stick to their guns, but at the same time they are confident enough to ask for help and realize the importance of collaboration in achieving their purpose."

Belief in Your Vision

As with belief in yourself, a passionate belief in your vision rubs off on those you lead. When your belief is high, their commitment rises to meet it. Great leaders know that at times their vision and goals will be challenged. The vision might even need to change or be readjusted. COVID-19 was a time when many organizations had to reset. Leaders with their eyes on a long-term goal can handle this. Whatever your vision may be, staying focused on it helps keep your team moving forward when facing difficult and unforeseeable obstacles. You must believe that temporary challenges cannot be viewed as permanent barriers. Your team must believe it, too.

One example of belief in vision and overcoming adverse situations comes from a Scottish football club I worked with in 2020 and 2021 during the lockdown. The club's academy director, Scott Allison had invited me to speak at the club and to the players on the Partick Thistle FC. They were lying 6th in the Scottish League One division in February 2021—far away from a promotion chance. Under figures such as Chief Executive Gerry Britton and team manager Ian McCall, the club developed a relentless drive and ambition to be promoted. Through unity and a strong belief in their vision, less than 3 months later, Partick Thistle was crowned 2020/2021 Scottish League One Champions. The team had used the lockdown as a positive to drive their culture and push for the title.

Belief in Your People

Letting your people know that you believe in them is usually the catalyst for them to believe in themselves. When you genuinely believe in someone, you lead them differently. You hold them to a higher standard. When they know that you believe in them, something in them changes. They begin to see what is possible. The voice of doubt in their head gets quieter, as the voice of inner belief gets louder.

If you want those you lead to believe in you as a leader or coach, you have to show them that you believe in them first. The more you believe in them, the more they believe in you and in themselves, which allows you to have more faith in them: It is a priceless upward spiral.

During my more active days coaching athletes, a large part of my philosophy was to intentionally instill self-belief and feed self-confidence in those I worked with. I was mindful of when and how I did that. This is not to say that I did not critique them, but remember that if you offer too much criticism, you jeopardize and even undermine their self-confidence, the opposite of a leader's job. Especially when it comes to working with kids, the most important four words they need to hear are "I believe in you." Regardless of age, we all need someone in our lives who believes in us.

Showing belief in those you lead is the hallmark of true leadership. Inspiring, challenging, coaching, guiding, correcting, and encouraging individuals to achieve their full potential is a responsibility of all leaders. Furthermore, I believe that it's one of the most fulfilling aspects of being a leader.

Who coaches you? Who's in your corner? Who believes in you, holds you accountable and helps you to reach your full potential? If you don't have a coach or mentor, do yourself a favor and find one. I can attest to the fact that the most effective leaders do just that.

SELF-REFLECTION TIME

- ◎ What leaders can you think of who have a high level of self-belief?
- ◎ What are some ways, in addition to telling them, to show that you believe in them?

"Outstanding leaders go out of their way to boost the self-esteem of their personnel. If people believe in themselves, it's amazing what they can accomplish."

– Sam Walton

CHAPTER 14

Lead with Adaptability

A dapt or perish, the old saying goes. Change happens. You must be able to face it and embrace it.

The key to adaptability is being open-minded and taking oneself out of autopilot to shift into curiosity. Is it time to reevaluate my vision? Is it time to rethink my planned course of action? Great leaders have the ability to change—or be changed—to fit new or unexpected circumstances. It is an essential skill for a leader because, as we know, the only thing constant in life is change itself. Leaders who are not willing to evolve and grow eventually find that their followers have become disillusioned, discouraged, disconnected—and possibly gone.

The COVID-19 pandemic was a world-wide example of leadership being challenged. We could see which leaders were better prepared and more solution-minded—and which ones weren't. The organizations and businesses that were able to survive and even thrive were the ones whose leaders were able to adapt their thinking and strategies.

While the fitness, hospitality and retail industries were among the hardest hit, home exercise equipment businesses like Peloton and meal delivery services like Hello Fresh flourished.

Other industries that rocketed during the pandemic included cleaning, tutoring, tech and healthcare, to name a few. Upon closer inspection, however, because of poor leadership, not all organizations in those industries necessarily enjoyed or maintained success. Those leaders and company owners who didn't act and adapt quickly fell behind. Sadly, so did many of their people.

The legendary Mike Krzyzewski, better known as Coach K, has been head basketball coach at Duke University since 1980 and has coached USA teams to consecutive gold medals at the 2008, 2012 and 2016 Summer Olympics. When I was consulting on the Duke University campus, I was fortunate enough to spend some time chatting with him in his office below the bleachers of the famous Cameron Indoor Stadium court.

Surrounded by countless trophies, memorabilia and awe-inspiring photos of Coach K with former presidents, superstar athletes and celebrities, I asked him what he felt were the most important traits in a great leader and coach. Leaning back into his chair, taking a pause as he often does, he cited adaptability. He said that it is not only a key to being a good leader or coach, but it is one of the keys to success in life. I might add that it is also necessary for a basketball player running up the basketball court.

He pointed to a cabinet in the corner of the office and said, "Allistair, do you see that file cabinet there? It has 40 seasons [yes, that's 40 years] of training programs in it. Not one of those is the same as another. Every single year has been different because some of the players change, and I have to adapt to them. No two players are alike. The way I engage and communicate with a Grant Hill, for example, will be different from how I am with a Zion Williamson." Every year college seniors graduate and new high school graduates enter Duke as freshmen—and every year Coach K adapts to the new members and new circumstances of his team.

Another great example of evolving and adapting is Phil Neville, the former Manchester United and England soccer player. In a conversation with him about celebrated Manchester United manager Sir Alex Ferguson, he mentioned that one of the things that made Sir

Alex so good at what he did was that he was always changing to suit the times. It was the reason he was able to be a successful manager for over 26 years at the club.

In my earlier years, when I was working as a Sports Performance Coach, I had the privilege of traveling the world and visiting many different countries, and I was able to experience many different cultures. I believe one of the main reasons I was successful in attracting and maintaining such high-profile clients as Olympic gold medalists, world champions and world #1-ranked athletes was my willingness to adapt to them and connect with them. For example, whatever country they were from, I made a concerted effort to learn some of their language and understand how things were done in their country.

It was through the simple practices of learning to understand them better and being adaptable that I was able to have a deeper connection with them. Looking back, I believe that if I had been more closed-minded and not willing to embrace their ways, I probably would not have had such a successful career in that field.

Another area where a leader has to be willing to embrace change is in dealing with different generations. For example, how you interact and communicate with Gen X is different from how you interact and communicate with Gen Z. In other words, if you aren't willing to adapt to your followers as a leader, you will struggle to make an impact or to get any buy-in from them at all. I believe that the leaders and coaches who are thriving the best today are the ones who first learn who their people are and then make the effort to really connect with them.

To be a leader who has influence and makes the intended impact means that you can't be close-minded or stuck in the past. What worked 10 years ago might not work today. What motivated your team last year might not motivate and inspire them this time around. The keys are that you evolve, stay creative and keep adapting.

Another coach who has earned great success is Mauricio Pochettino. The Argentinian coach spent 5 years at the English club Tottenham Hotspurs before moving to Paris Saint-Germain FC. Two of the reasons he was successful there were his man-management skills and that he was able to adapt to each player. In an interview, Pochettino shared that he was always finding ways to stay current and relatable to his players and staff. He remained open-minded, and the players who worked under him loved and responded to that.

Successful leaders are adaptable and non-judgmental. They are lifelong learners who wake up each day with a hunger to learn and understand more. Remember the famous quote from General Eric Shinseki: "If you dislike change, you're going to dislike irrelevance even more." Great leaders adapt to new people, new environments, and new circumstances.

SELF-REFLECTION TIME

- As a leader, can you give an example of when you had to change or adapt to a new situation or person?
- Give one or two examples of how you feel you are evolving.

"As a leader, you have to keep adapting and changing...not your values, but how you get your message across."

– Mike Krzyzewski

CHAPTER 15

Lead with Buy-In

A question I'm often asked is, "How do I get buy-in from those I lead?" Buy-in occurs when the team members choose to support the leader and the organization's vision and objectives. They are committed to what has been asked of them.

When I asked Phil Jones MBE, the Managing Director of Brother Technologies in the UK, how buy-in is created, he explained it like this: "It's the decisions, actions and behaviors you demonstrate as a leader over time. These are key to developing trust with colleagues and remain core components of the buy-in process. Never forget the "why?" within the "what?" so that everyone can fully understand decisions about your proposed direction. Ensure your communications are clear, unambiguous and delivered in a way that visuals and words amplify your message effectively. A buy-in doesn't always mean 100 percent agreement, but if it means 100 percent support, then job done."

It's almost impossible to achieve a culture of collaboration and excellence without buy-in. Dallas Eakins, head coach of the NHL Hockey team the Anaheim Ducks (not to be confused with the University of Oregon Ducks), put it well. "Team culture is not bought; it's caught. It's very hard to make people do things. It's easier to inspire them, and that's how you eventually create a buy-in."

5 Elements of Buy-in

1. Vision
2. Character
3. Inclusion
4. Support
5. Communication

The first element in buy-in is **vision.** Leaders lay out the vision and show their team where they are today and where they should be tomorrow. It is important that every person on the team feels a part of the vision. A vision is a destination; if your team doesn't know exactly where they are going, they cannot buy in.

The second element is **character**. People buy into leadership based in large part on the character of the person in charge. Only after that will they buy into the vision. Moreover, in order for the leader to get the best from them, team members expect the person in charge to have honesty and commitment, to demonstrate integrity, to maintain organization standards and to create a culture of openness.

The third element is **inclusion** in decision making. Buy-in won't happen if it's only the leader making the decisions. Team members want their voices to be heard. Stephen Covey, author of the best-selling book *The Seven Habits of Highly Effective People*, suggests that inclusion is a prerequisite for commitment. Leaders should involve team members in the decision making process. When a leader includes team members' input, they feel a co-ownership that inspires commitment. In fact, it's something that NBA basketball coaches like Greg Popovich of the San Antonio Spurs and Steve Kerr of the Golden State Warriors believe in whole heartedly. Both coaches sometimes step back and hand over the coaching roles and decision making to the players themselves.

The fourth element is **support.** It's one thing to get a buy-in from the beginning, but how do you sustain it? A great leader must be able to support, guide and motivate their people throughout a project or mission. For you to sustain your people's buy-in, they need to know that you are there every step of the way.

They want you to listen to them, offer and receive feedback, encourage, and be prepared to compromise when necessary. Buy-in itself is often lost if team members lose faith in their leaders' support because they think the leader is overcritical, changes their mind too often or doesn't show commitment. Great leaders cultivate support when they recognize and reward processes and small goals achieved along the way, not just the final result.

The final element is **communication.** When you provide clear and honest communication, team members feel well informed and motivated to stay on the same page. Lack of consistent communication leads to confusion, disfunction, distrust and detachment. Many great leaders like to overcommunicate (repeat their message), and they encourage their team members to do so as well.

Leaders lay out a vision and demonstrate character in order to motivate and nurture support from their people. Consistent and transparent communication maintain a culture that enables and fosters buy-in.

SELF-REFLECTION TIME

- ◎ As a leader, how important do you feel it is to have buy-in from those you lead? Why?

- ◎ What do you believe is the hardest aspect of getting and maintaining buy-in from those you lead?

"Team culture is not bought; it's caught. It's very hard to make people do things. It's easier to inspire them, and that's how you eventually create a buy-in."

– Dallas Eakins

CHAPTER 16

Lead with Humor

I'm pretty sure you've heard the saying "Laughter is the best medicine." A Bell Leadership Institute study found that a sense of humor is one of the most desirable traits in leaders. Nearly all of us enjoy being around someone who has a great sense of humor and makes us smile. Thinking back, I bet you remember the coaches, teachers, managers or leaders you've had who did this. I certainly do.

Surveys of different demographic populations reveal the power of humor. According to a Robert Half survey, 91 percent of executives believe that a sense of humor is important for career advancement, and 84 percent believe that those with a good sense of humor do a better job. When people can see the funny side of things, the atmosphere is lightened and more relaxed. Furthermore, in leaders, humor and humility seem to go hand in hand. They are a counterbalance for self-confidence, something that keeps leaders' feet on the ground and their egos in check.

A survey I conducted in 2018 involved student athletes from 8 different colleges around the United States. One question I asked was this: From a list of 10 options, what are the top 3 qualities you look for in a coach? Of the 118 athletes, more than 75 percent listed humor in their top 3 traits. Humor is certainly among a coach's most effective tools.

From executives to students, people view humor as a strong attribute and motivator.

What I have discovered in working with many organizations, both corporate and sports, is that leaders with a sense of humor usually build more cohesive cultures and more enjoyable work environments, both of which promote buy-in and productivity. Especially in times of adversity or stress, a leader can use humor to relieve tension and allow team members to focus on solutions instead of problems. Moreover, cultures that incorporate humor enjoy the benefits of more resilience and more of a feeling of togetherness.

Jokes and wit help relieve stress and lift the moods and motivation of the team. In his book *The Humor Advantage*, international business speaker and author Michael Kerr explains how humor is a valuable tension breaker in the workplace. Laughter increases the endorphins released by the brain, relieves stress and relaxes the muscles. People who see a lighter side in response to a conflict tend to shift from convergent thinking that focuses on only one solution to divergent thinking where multiple ideas expand the possibilities.

I've discovered that in the teams and organizations I have visited, where there is shared humor, the atmosphere is always happier and more energetic. Humor is also something that can relieve nerves, stress and anxiety. One example is a university I consult at in Louisiana. When I was there recently, one team member mentioned that before going out to compete, the team used to be nervous, doubtful, and low in energy. He described the dressing room before a match as feeling much like a funeral. Then one day a team member decided to introduce music, humor and more fun into the dressing room before the team went out to compete. The result was that the players felt less doubtful, more energized and more confident.

One of my favorite authors and podcast hosts is James Altucher. James has founded or cofounded over 20 companies and has published no less than 20 books. Altucher believes that humor in the workplace is a great leveler and way to win people over. In addition, he often uses it to lighten up tense situations.

According to a report from St. Edward's University, an Australian study of 2,500 employees found that 81 percent believed a fun working environment would make them more productive; 93 percent said that laughing on the job helped to reduce work-related stress. This can be true in any work environment. When I see a winning team, whether sports or corporate, I see a team that is having fun. They work hard with focus and intensity, but there's a healthy banter and a great energy about them.

On the flip side, we have to be cautious that humor or joking doesn't become nasty or too personal. Then it is no longer funny. Over-the-top banter or biting sarcasm has a negative effect on individuals and the group, and, in fact, can create a toxic environment. Avoid this. Humor at the expense of someone's feelings is not humor. It is meanness. A person who tries to pass their meanness off as humor kills morale, creates a toxic atmosphere and depresses productivity. Don't allow this.

There is also the scenario where someone is using "humor" and doesn't realize they are being hurtful. A few years back I was consulting at a prominent basketball program at a college in the United States. As I usually do, I got to spend one-on-one time with the players. In these sessions they are able to share their experiences, issues and concerns with me. Out of the 15 players, 9 brought up the fact that they didn't appreciate their coach's sarcasm. Even though they all agreed he was a great coach and they knew that he cared for them, they felt his supposed humor belittled them. We should always be aware of what we are saying and, even more, how we are saying it, as this coach discovered.

Valorie Kondos Field, one of the most successful gymnastics coaches in the history of NCAA college sports, brought up the subject of humor-that-isn't-funny on an episode of my podcast. "Miss Val," as she's known to her athletes, has coached several Olympians, including Madison Kocian, Kyla Ross and Jordyn Wieber, and led UCLA to 7 National titles. She admitted that in her earlier coaching days she had at times been hurtfully sarcastic. One day she was summoned to an urgent meeting called by her athletes. One by one, they provided her with examples of the things she had said to them that had been hurtful. Coach Val listened, didn't interrupt and thanked the girls. From that day on, she changed her approach. And from that day on, she has held their much deserved respect.

Leading with a healthy sense of humor relieves stress, enhances problem-solving skills, elevates the moods of others, creates a new perspective, fosters better communication and improves cooperation and empathy among people. All from one attitude adjustment. People relate to each other more positively if the environment includes a healthy sense of humor.

Take advantage of its many benefits. It can help you create a healthy, uplifting and productive environment.

SELF-REFLECTION TIME

- As a leader, in what ways do you think a sense of humor helps in the workplace?

- As a leader, can you think of a time when your "humor" was over the top? What did you do about it?

"A sense of humor is part of the art of leadership, of getting along with people, of getting things done."

– Dwight D. Eisenhower

CHAPTER 17

Lead with Optimism

One trait I've discovered in great leaders and influencers is that they are optimists. They are the glass-half-full type and believe that the impossible is possible. Think about some pioneers in their fields: airplane inventors the Wright brothers, Apple's Steve Jobs, Virgin's Richard Branson, Amazon's Jeff Bezos or Space-X's Elon Musk. They all lead (or led) with vision, courage and optimism.

These "explorers," as I like to refer to them, are (or were) leaders who have had an enormous impact in their chosen fields—and in the world—and relentlessly pursued their goals. Like all great leaders, they showed up with optimism in spite of countless failures and naysayers. They showed up with confidence. They showed up with energy. They showed up with curiosity. They showed up prepared. They showed up ready to lead.

I believe that optimism is essential to great leadership. The best leaders I have encountered in my career were or are those who remain, ambitious and optimistic. Their optimism enables them to recognize the potential in situations and in people when others do not.

As a leader, you're required to present a vision for your people. No matter what the obstacles, your people are looking to you to show strong character, composure and faith in your goals. No matter the situation, how great the obstacle or the odds are, optimistic leaders believe that the best outcomes are always possible.

Pessimistic leaders, on the other hand, bring a grey cloud wherever they go. They predict the worst. They complain, blame others and usually play the victims. They have a tendency to spread their negative energy to those around them. They see challenges as problems instead of as opportunities. How much time do you want to spend around these people?

Optimistic leaders have a certain energy that attracts others to them. They have the ability to keep going despite hurdles that pop up. Optimists know how to make the most of the inspiring power of their positive outlook—they are aware of the fact that their energy is contagious and want to spread it those who look to them for direction and energy.

Some of you who are lovers of sports commercials might remember a few years back when actor Jason Sudeikis made a series of ads promoting NBC's English Premier League Soccer programming. Now returning in the Amazon+ series *Ted Lasso*, Sudeikis plays Lasso, a twangy American football coach who has somehow become head coach of the English club Tottenham Hotspurs. He knows next to nothing about the game and has to deal with many forms of culture shock, but he never loses his positive outlook. In the face of enormous resistance, he wins his people over by remaining persistently optimistic.

It can be no surprise that optimistic leaders are more successful than their pessimistic counterparts: They have excellent coping skills and higher levels of emotional intelligence. They are not afraid to make on-the-spot decisions. They aim to solve problems and improve whatever situation they find themselves in. They take more risks and are more resilient when facing failure and setbacks in life—because they see it all as part of the adventurous journey. They are "can-do" people.

Speaker, writer, and entrepreneur Dr. Tommy Weir observed, "An optimistic leader describes what can be achieved. They talk about it. They're excited about it. They inspire others to see success coming.

And more so, they give their teams a reason to embrace this belief." The people Weir is describing are comfortable thinking outside the box; in fact, that is where they are at their happiest and most fulfilled. They enjoy solving problems and like to ask questions from different perspectives. For instance, when seeking solutions, they ask, *What is needed?* (instead of *What is wrong?*), What it going well? (instead of *What is going badly?*), and *What steps can be taken to work toward implementing the solution?* (instead of sitting dormant on the problem).

Nowhere is optimism more important than in leading people and organizations. Highly effective leaders have the skill of being able to convince others that they have the ability to achieve levels of performance beyond those they thought possible. Their optimism prompts them to show those they lead not what they are, but what they can become.

When the people in charge live and practice optimism, they create and nurture long-term relationships with their team members and with others. They know the importance of engaging and motivating others. No matter how turbulent things may be, optimistic leaders stay focused on the big picture: They visualize and believe in a better tomorrow—and in making the impossible a reality.

SELF-REFLECTION TIME

- ◎ As a leader, how optimistic and positive are you, especially in more challenging and difficult times?
- ◎ Do you think that those under your leadership view you as optimistic?

"What I've learned over time is that optimism is a very, very important part of leadership."

– Bob Iger

CHAPTER 18

Lead with Consistency

A culture of excellence requires habits of consistency. Without consistency, growth and success cannot happen. The importance of consistency has the attention of Dwayne "The Rock" Johnson. "Success isn't always about greatness. It's about consistency. Consistent hard work leads to success. Greatness will come." He knows what he's talking about—he was the highest paid male actor two years in a row.

When I hear the word consistency, I think about self-discipline. If you really want to achieve success, expect to make it a way of life. Consistently: Show up, put in the work, give your best, have no regrets.

Russell Wilson, the Superbowl-winning quarterback of the Seattle Seahawks, understands the connection between leadership, self-discipline and consistency. "I think the way I view leadership and playing in the quarterback position is that you got to be consistent every single day in terms of watching film, in terms of being there and getting there on time. You have got to make sure you're working your butt off in the weight room, and then when you're on the sideline talking to your guys, you are having great communication. I'm determined to be successful and that's what I try to bring to the table. To be a great leader you have to be consistent every single day and set the example for the rest."

There is a reason why the world's best performers in their fields achieved that status. Whether it's in the sports, entertainment or corporate world, the best of the best stay consistent. Some days they might make big gains, some days they might make smaller ones, but what they grasp, like Johnson and Wilson, is that your work ethic—based on consistency—elevates you and serves as a solid role model to those who look up to you.

If you look around, you will see that the reason most people fall short of achieving their personal greatness isn't due to lack of knowledge, talent or ability, but rather due to lack of purpose, self-discipline and consistency. For example, if you were to ask me for advice on writing a book, I would say that it's not easy and it requires consistency. Write a little bit every day, even just a page! It doesn't matter if it's bad or good; it doesn't matter if you're in the mood or not, feeling inspired or having a bad day. What ultimately matters is that you're consistently showing up and trying. You can apply this strategy to any of your goals.

Ben Ryan is the Rio Olympic gold medal winning coach with the Fijian 7s rugby team. Ben is a good friend and one of the world's best in the business. I asked him about the importance of staying consistent as a leader. He believes that little things reveal a lot. "As a leader, it's the small consistent actions and words that measure your leadership and the trust of those around you. It's the small, consistent behaviors that show you care, creating a climate where those you coach and those you work with can rely on how you act, how you react and how you behave. *Consistently*. When the pressure is on, you can still be your best version, serving those around you." He cautioned, "Don't be that coach who high fives an athlete after they have scored a winning goal, and then the next week ignores them when they get sent off the field. If you want to build real, lasting trust, you have to build you own consistent actions and behaviors."

Dean Smith, manager/coach of the English football club Aston Villa, knew the importance of consistency in leadership from the beginning. "One of the biggest things I want to be is consistent with the players. They need to see consistency from the person making the decisions. When I first came into coaching, I said to myself, 'I want to be a manager who I would have wanted to be managed by.' I live by that statement every day."

Building trust and credibility doesn't happen overnight. The more consistent you are as a leader over a period of time, the more you earn. Your steadiness provides reassurance for your people. Your faith in them gives them more faith in themselves. And the next thing you know, you are enjoying more favorable and reliable outcomes.

Great leaders build consistency in the relationships and connections they have with others. They are reliable on a daily basis, checking in on their people and bringing a positive energy with them, despite—or perhaps because of—inevitable challenges.

Consistency in a leader helps develop routines and build momentum. It forms habits that become second nature. Russell Wilson and Dwayne "The Rock" Johnson credit consistency with helping them rise to the top. Let it help you.

SELF-REFLECTION TIME

- ◎ As a leader, in what ways are you consistent?
- ◎ When it comes to your leadership skills, in what areas do you feel you could improve your consistency?

"Success isn't always about greatness. It's about consistency. Consistent hard work leads to success."

– Dwayne Johnson

CHAPTER 19

Lead with Self-Leadership

W hile leadership focuses on how one influences others, self-leadership is about observing and managing oneself. Team members must see your solid self-leadership skills before they can believe in your organization leadership skills.

Self-leadership is about developing and managing your energy and drive so that you can stay motivated and perform at your highest level. It encompasses everything from how you wake up and conduct your morning routine to the strategies you use to keep your daily life organized and flowing. It is, in fact, the subject I spend the most time on with the leaders and people I mentor.

Leadership is about serving others, so it's only natural that many leaders spend the majority of their time focusing on external responsibilities like directing people and projects. As head basketball coach George Raveling noted, "While one of the greatest joys of leadership is helping others achieve what they never thought possible, we will not give others our best selves if we do not manage how we think and live first." So how often do you spend time focusing on managing yourself?

Cultivate and maintain an honest understanding of who you are, where you want to go and what you can accomplish. Learn to manage your emotions and behavior in a way that guides you toward your goals. Proactively take charge of your growth and development.

Daniel Goleman, author of the 1992 best-seller *Emotional Intelligence*, noted that exceptional leaders distinguish themselves through superior self-leadership.

That is, the very best leaders excel at *leading themselves*. Before your people buy into your capabilities, they first buy into the person you are.

Self-leadership can be broken down into 4 areas:

1. **Self-awareness:** Great leaders know themselves. It can be hard to admit your weaknesses and flaws to yourself, but what is even harder to face is the fact that your people may know them better than you do. Take the time to acknowledge and to understand your behaviors, perspectives, strengths and limiting factors. A great way to start is to reflect on your day each evening. What did you do well and how can you improve?

2. **Self-management:** Because great leaders self-manage well, they are more focused and more productive. They practice self-discipline. Hold yourself accountable for how you control your time, actions and resources. Although it's not always easy, prioritize the elements of your life in such a way that each one gets the attention it deserves.

3. **Social awareness:** Great leaders stay mindful of what is happening around them. This is a place where emotional intelligence (EQ) is priceless. If EQ is not a strength of yours, work on it. Notice what others say and what they are feeling. Empathize. You will reap big rewards in surprising ways. Legendary football manager, Sir Alex Ferguson, believed that one of the most important skills a leader should have is the power of observation. "In constantly listening to and watching others, you can understand the crux of who they are—where they came from and what makes them who they are today. Watching people is key to picking up small details. When you are more in tune with how each person is feeling, you can make better decisions."

4. **Social management:** Great leaders have developed their interpersonal skills. Help your people overcome challenges

and deal with conflict. Learn what motivates them and help them realize their full potential. Wise social management paves the way to achieving your organization's objectives with the fewest possible bumps in the road.

Effective self-leadership doesn't happen by accident. Pay consistent attention to self-awareness, self-reflection and self-discipline. Find an agreeable, organized and consistent daily routine. Identify your goals and manage your actions and your interactions with others in ways that inspire them to work well with you and with each other. You will be more productive and inspire others to follow your lead.

SELF-REFLECTION TIME

- ◎ How much time do you spend on developing and leading yourself?
- ◎ Which areas within your self-leadership skill set do you feel require more attention?

"Before you are a leader, success is about growing yourself. When you become a leader, success is about growing others."

– Jack Welch

CHAPTER 20

Lead with Compassion

Countries around the globe became united in efforts to stop the spread of COVID-19, which has claimed millions of lives—more than anyone imagined possible. It's devastating.

In addition, millions lost their jobs, meaning that they might not be able to pay bills and might fall behind professionally. Within my own circle, three friends had to close their businesses and lay off their employees. It's the hardest thing they have ever had to do, and it's heart wrenching to witness.

During this time, we have been exposed to all kinds of leadership in the political, educational, sports, medical and essential-services industries. What has been fascinating to observe is how various leaders have responded to pandemic and crisis. Many have risen to the occasion. One fact that strikes me is this: The leaders who have led with purpose and made an impact have been those who have displayed compassion and a deep understanding of what people need.

When I think of compassionate leaders over time, St. Francis of Assisi, Mahatma Gandhi, Nelson Mandela, Mother Theresa and, in more recent times, Jacinda Ardern spring to mind. Most of these role models have been gone for years or even centuries, yet we still remember them for their grand scale compassion.

In sports, I have discovered that the coaches with higher levels of concern for their fellow human beings succeed better in the long run. Coaches who show empathy for the feelings of their athletes provide a strong—and valuable—support system. In a conversation I had with Patrick Mourataglou, the longtime coach of Serena Williams, he said that he believes compassionate coaches have an ability to understand what their athletes are going through and are therefore best able to help them. Compassionate coaches listen in order to understand, not merely to respond, he emphasized. They also recognize that they don't need to have solutions and answers all the time, just a willing ear. They see the value in the person more than just in the player, and they show it.

Some of the best coaches weren't necessarily elite level players. Rather, in addition to having a complete understanding of their sport, they are compassionate and insightful people who are able to get full potential from their clients. Playing a sport and teaching or coaching it are two entirely different skill sets.

An equally important facet of compassion is compassion for yourself. When you are under stress, let your team members know from your example that it's okay to cut themselves some slack without going overboard. Even for great leaders, it's impossible to have all the right answers all the time.

Compassion gives us the ability to step outside of ourselves and better understand someone else's situation and, beyond that, to take action to improve their lives.

Moreover, compassion lifts people up. It encourages, praises, inspires and embraces the humanity of others. Having compassion is more than just an act of leadership; it is a way of life.

SELF-REFLECTION TIME

- ◎ How do you show compassion as a leader?
- ◎ Why do you think having compassion is important for a leader?

"The purpose of human life is to serve and to show compassion and the will to help others."

– Dr. Albert Schweitzer

CHAPTER 21

Lead with Communication Skills

C larity in communication is an essential factor in cultivating a synergistic culture within your team.

If this already makes sense to you, you know that it gains you trust, drives your vision, provides specific direction, clarifies expectations and helps team members work with efficiency and confidence. In addition, clear communication sets the standard for a culture of accountability and trust.

If you don't see the importance, imagine an NFL football game with no huddles to let the players know what the quarterback has planned for his probable 67-84 plays. Or imagine firefighters arriving at a fire and there's no officer telling them where to go or what equipment they need—and the fire is at your house.

In an *INC.* magazine article published in January 2021, a look into 400 companies with at least 100,000 employees found that those companies lost, on average, $62.4 million annually due to poor communication. Smaller companies may not lose such big sums, but the cost of miscommunication affects their bottom line more acutely.

The more effective the communication, the better understanding everyone will have. When communication is lacking or inconsistent, important information can be misinterpreted, destructive actions can be taken and frustrated team members will be saying imprudent things—all barriers that hinder progress.

Even if it doesn't come naturally, leaders should be skilled at speaking. Fortunately, it is an ability that can be learned. Although some people might say that I look comfortable when I'm onstage speaking, I had to go through a certain amount of discomfort working to improve. Even the great Zig Ziglar acknowledged that in his first few years he wasn't comfortable speaking to large groups. People told him that he was a natural, but that wasn't actually the case. As we know, Zig became one of the most influential inspirational speakers ever, but he had to work at it. A bonus is that developing your public speaking skills will serve you well in many unforeseeable areas of life. The effort is well worth it.

Effective speaking does not come naturally for most people. Many, including leaders and coaches, had to do a lot of practicing to sharpen their skills. If you aren't good at communicating in front of groups, my advice is simply to get better. Invest in your speaking skills; for example, you could hire a speech coach. I have read books and watched videos of some of the world's best speakers and have spent countless hours in front of mirrors and friends practicing my speaking skills. Again, all well worth the effort.

Darcy Norman, former head of Performance at Roma Football club in Italy, believes that effective communication is key in developing and working with elite teams. "We can convey a message in many different ways, which influences how well we interact." Great leaders and coaches are able to adapt their communication styles to suit the person or group they are communicating with. A primary rule of speaking is to know your audience.

Clarity on the part of its leader improves an organization's ability to execute tasks and deliver results because its people have confidence in what they are doing. In addition, better communication builds collaboration and trust.

Did you know that one of the most powerful forms of communication is actually not talking, but listening? Effective communicators know when to talk and, more importantly, when to listen. Stay in the moment and avoid interrupting. I find that the more

I listen and the less I talk, the more I learn and the better I understand the other party. As I mentioned earlier about the 80/20 communicator, I try to listen 80 percent of the time and talk only 20 percent.

The American author Ernest Hemingway once said, "When people talk, listen completely. Don't be thinking about what you're going to say. Most people never listen. Nor do they observe." The practice of listening and observing gave Hemingway the insights to create many memorable characters.

This willingness to listen and observe is the reason some of the most adept communicators are also skilled in sensing the moods, energy, attitudes, values and concerns of those they are communicating with. They pay attention not only to the words but also to the actions and non-verbal cues that accompany them. Great speakers read their environment well and adjust their communication style to the current situation. They are making use of high emotional intelligence.

Do not be afraid that you will overcommunicate. (Note: Whether your words are spoken or written, this is not permission to prattle on endlessly.) From very early in my career, if there was going to be a meeting Friday at 9 a.m., I sent an email reminder a few days beforehand, then on the day before and on the morning of the meeting. I wanted no misunderstandings or excuses.

Let me take a moment to address the subject of email communication. When most people open an email, the first thing they do is scroll down to see how long it is. Then they decide if they are going to read it now. If the email is longer than a few lines, many people leave it for later—or maybe never.

Here are a few guidelines to getting your emails opened, read and acted on:

1. Make good use of subject lines.
2. Keep messages short and to the point.

3. Explain the reason for the email in the first or second line.

4. Insert spaces between paragraphs for easier reading.

5. Use bullets points.

6. If you need an answer, make it known and by when.

7. Check spelling and proofread before hitting Send.

Let's get back to overcommunication. Patrick Lencioni, leadership expert and author of the book *The Five Dysfunctions of a Team*, writes, "I'll admit, I'm an over communicator. In fact, sometimes my kids will tease me about it. They'll say, 'Dad, if you tell me that one more time!' The people at the office will say, 'Yeah, yeah, Patrick, we got it!' Sometimes I'll feel bad that maybe I'm communicating too much, but I think it's better to have a family, an organization or company where people are clear than have situations where people don't really understand. Don't be afraid to overcommunicate; the fact that you're repeating things means there will be more clarity. The Australian Philanthropist Samuel Johnson said, 'People need to be reminded more than they need to be instructed. I love that.'"

In a study published in the *Harvard Business Review*, thirteen managers were observed and their communication was tracked. The findings were that when communication is repeated, it is more likely that a project will be completed more quickly and with fewer mistakes. It's far better to convey information too many times than too few.

When you communicate with the people in your organization, first remember the purpose of your message, and second the makeup of your audience. Have you made it a point to listen to and observe them? Consider if, when and how the message should be repeated. Make clarity in communication work for you.

SELF-REFLECTION TIME

- As a leader, how would you describe your style of communicating?
- In what particular areas do you feel you could improve your communication skills?

"To effectively communicate, we must realize that we are all different in the way we perceive the world and use this understanding as a guide to our communication with others."

– Anthony Robbins

CHAPTER 22

Lead with Healthy Confrontation

The word *confrontation* is usually associated with something negative. However, a successful and productive culture requires healthy confrontation. The pivotal word here is *healthy*.

Issues and problems must be addressed, but confrontation should be respectful and mutually beneficial and make people better individually as team members and better collectively as a team.

Most of the successful organizations I've worked with embrace confrontation in a beneficial and productive manner. My good friend and former head of performance at Paris Saint-Germain Football Club Martin Buchheit wrote in his book *EGOals* (co-written with George Perry): "The ability to talk openly and to not leave things under the carpet is key, and everything that can be said or done early to prevent the situation escalating is always welcome. I tend as much as I can to have those open discussions with as much humility and empathy as possible to defuse potential bombs, but the reality is that not many people are ready to have those discussions."

Whether or not people are ready to have these discussions, issues and disagreements will arise from time to time. But the outcomes depend on how directly and how tactfully they are handled. Speaking on the subject of healthy confrontation, Tony Smith, the Australian rugby league coach, said, "I don't expect people to walk around giving out bouquets of flowers and it's all happy days. There need to be some disagreements and differing opinions, but what matters is how those things are conveyed to one another. It's being able to communicate without losing control. It's having decency. We talk about that a lot when we have our team meetings. We want to make sure that everyone can be heard and be respected when they speak. It's young players being confident to speak in meetings, and knowing their opinions are valued."

Avoidance of constructive confrontation is probably one of the greatest contributing factors to the failures of leaders and cultures. When the hard conversations aren't being had, and the hard issues aren't being properly addressed, that's an issue.

I recently read an insightful quote from an executive director at a large American bank. She said, "In most organizations, people will shut down when opposing ideas are not allowed, and you have a false sense of agreement that everything is going well. People won't share thoughts and feelings. When you shut down disagreement, you shut down creativity and end up with the ability to fail fast."

Bill Parcells was head coach of the NFL New York Giants, the New England Patriots, the New York Jets and the Dallas Cowboys. During his 19 seasons he twice won the Superbowl as head coach. Parcells believes that when he started at the Giants, he lacked the confidence and ability to confront the star players on the team. As a result, he didn't get their respect and wasn't able to make an impact. They had a dismal season and Parcells felt he would most certainly be fired at the end. So when he wasn't, he figured that he had nothing to lose and changed his leadership style.

Parcells decided to be more straightforward, even with star players. "If you want to get the most out of people, you have to apply pressure. I've found that people want the direct approach, as long as it's done in a respectful way. It's much more valuable to have a leader who's absolutely clear and open than to have one who soft-soaps or talks in circles."

Leadership in many workplaces needs to change the way it approaches confrontation. In healthy organizations and team cultures, positive confrontation is routine because they recognize that it is a necessity to maintaining their strength.

Particularly in a team environment, you can't lead effectively if you are unwilling to give appropriate feedback to team members when their behavior interferes with the goals and objectives of the team. Why then is there such a stigma attached to confrontation? It is, of course, because of our generally negative history with it. Confrontation doesn't have to be a negative if managed correctly.

When you are dealing with confrontation, the intension should never be to belittle or shame another person, but to come to a suitable agreement. Well run organizations provide the skills and guidelines to their people about how to approach and manage challenging situations so that disagreement resolution becomes constructive rather than destructive.

Great leaders are able to deliver bad news in a good way. This was the ability former Manchester United footballer Phil Neville spoke about when referring to the manner in which manager Sir Alex Ferguson delivered bad news. Phil explained to me that Sir Alex had a way of making you still feel good about yourself, even if you had been dropped from the team that week. "It's funny, but after receiving some bad news from Sir Alex, you would leave his office actually thanking him and being motivated to work harder moving forward. He made you feel valued and important."

If a team member is performing below the required standard, address it as soon as possible. When a leader doesn't take appropriate action, not only will the team suffer, but more detrimentally, trust will be lost in the leader. As former England international football player and Manchester United Women's head coach Casey Stoney told me, "I have always believed that trust is built from having the tough conversations, even though they're not easy at times. No one really likes having them, but they are necessary."

Usually what you'll find is that when you have a more open and candid culture, there will be fewer hard conversations necessary. In other words, consistent communication contributes to eliminating misunderstandings and conflict.

Author of the book *The Five Dysfunctions of a Team* Patrick Lencioni writes, "When you trust people, disagreement is the pursuit of truth. The best organizations generally have more disagreement due to less fear of the fallout from that disagreement." In such organizations, members feel less threatened to confront issues or have the tougher conversations. The key, of course, is approach. When it's done tactfully, the leader—and the organization—will enjoy more favorable outcomes.

Remember that spending time with people who are unlike you or who have different opinions and views is a great learning accelerator. We acquire the most knowledge when we encounter people who are the least like us. Resist the urge to avoid the confrontation conversation without first considering what you can gain from others.

4 Helpful Steps to Approaching the Hard Conversations

1. PREP—Before having the conversation, aim to get all the facts and be properly prepared. Jot down some points that can help you during the conversation.

2. DEFINE—Define your desired outcome from the conversation and anticipate what might be said and how the other person might react.

3. DIRECT—Be direct, but aim to control your emotions and body language.

4. DELIVER—When you are having a hard conversation, get your point across and finish at that. Don't linger with innocuous conversation because you feel guilty about delivering bad news. Once the issues have been discussed, end the meeting. Don't dilute all you just said by participating in conversation that distracts from your purpose.

Many people believe that starting and ending with positive words is the best way to approach these conversations. These are sometimes known as "s**t sandwiches." I don't endorse this approach. Start with pleasantries such as "Hi, thanks for taking the time to meet with me," etc., then address the issue courteously and close tactfully.

Healthy confrontation is necessary, and it can be constructive when you conduct it respectfully and with a plan.

SELF-REFLECTION TIME

- ◎ As a leader, how do you deal with conflict and confrontation?
- ◎ What do you feel can improve within your organization when dealing with conflict and confrontation?

"I have always believed that trust is built from having the tough conversations, even though they're not easy at times. No one really enjoys them, but they are necessary."

– Casey Stoney

CHAPTER 23

Lead with Vulnerability

It's easy to distinguish the kind of leader a person is by how much vulnerability they are willing to display. Evidence is growing that leaders who are more vulnerable and transparent with those they lead are more trusted and respected.

Starbucks founder and CEO Howard Schultz retired in 2000 and returned to that position in 2007 after the business experienced a substantial downturn. He believes in the value of vulnerability. "You have to be honest and authentic and not hide," he said. "I think today's leaders have to demonstrate both transparency and vulnerability, and with that comes truthfulness and humility." In fact, when Schultz rejoined the organization, he opened up with his employees and was transparent about his challenges and vulnerabilities, which helped drive a return to growth.

Being open and vulnerable is something that many people struggle with—and I speak from my own experience. Fortunately, over the years, I have been able to let go of trying to display a persona of perfection and competence in every area and have learned how to show my vulnerabilities and shortcomings more. I have also learned to ask for help in areas that I'm not as knowledgeable or competent in. This process, although incredibly scary and uncomfortable in the beginning, has been liberating and life changing. I just wish I'd done it earlier.

Brené Brown, author of the book *Dare to Lead*, defines vulnerability as uncertainty, risk and emotional exposure. Brené believes that vulnerability and leadership go hand in hand because both require us to take the risk of stepping forward and showing up in a form that exposes us.

Fear of vulnerability is closely linked to our ego and our insecurity. Usually, they are responsible for keeping us from allowing ourselves to be vulnerable. As leaders, we want to show our people that we are brave, competent and capable. We want to appear that we are in control, especially in the midst of a storm. However, like everyone else, we have our fears, flaws and limiting factors.

Something I've learned over the years is that people are more inspired by our shortcomings and our ability to overcome them than just by our successes and accomplishments. They are able to connect with us more easily. One of the things I changed when speaking to large groups was that instead of starting with an inspiring or personal success story, I now like to start with a story where I failed or messed up somewhere. Of course, I try keep it light. By adopting this approach, I feel my audience better relates to me and is able to see the more authentic side of me.

Being up-front and open with vulnerability is an important leadership quality. Being able to admit and share times of weakness, even in a public setting, is a way for leaders to earn trust from those they lead. When asked about this subject, former England football captain and Chelsea manager Frank Lampard observed, "The only way you can create a good environment is that when you're asking for everyone to be 100 percent responsible, they need to see that from the leader first. I don't think it's a problem to show weakness or vulnerability. I'm not afraid to admit when I'm wrong or I have messed up."

Vulnerable leaders are comfortable with not having all the answers or solutions. They are comfortable bringing other people into conversations to share their ideas and opinions. These leaders embrace the truth. They are more interested in understanding reality than in being right and are not afraid to accept when they are wrong. This allows them to welcome feedback and criticism because they know it's necessary in order to make progress.

Brené Brown believes that you can't be courageous without being vulnerable and that vulnerability and leadership go hand in hand. No leader has it all; when building trust with others, it's important to be authentic, open and honest.

Putting yourself on a pedestal and singing your own praises and successes does not prompt others to relate to you or trust you with their own limitations. Even though they might be impressed by what you have done, they want to know that you are both a human (just like them) and a leader they can make a connection with and relate to. People crave a leader who is real, who is willing to admit their faults and mistakes.

As I mentioned, I show vulnerability by using "moments"—relatable situations that share my shortcomings and blunders. I've found that by doing this, I have been able to create more trust and a safer environment that empower others to be more open and honest. When team members see that the leader is willing to share information honestly, the leader sends a strong message that this is not only acceptable throughout the organization, but it is the norm.

Some words of caution: Being vulnerable in front of others, especially strangers, can be risky. Let's recognize that there is a difference between being vulnerable and sharing too much information. Be prudent and sensible. Remember that when it comes to being vulnerable, especially in the workplace, there are certain people who don't deserve your vulnerability and openness; some people don't have your best interests at heart. Also, there is a time and place to be vulnerable. Especially in the beginning stages, you should aim to be strategic about what you disclose. Pouring your heart out in the very first meeting is probably not a wise choice as it will only make for an incredibly uncomfortable situation for everyone and could cause problems for you. The more that time passes and trust is formed, the more vulnerability you will be able to share with others.

Vulnerability allows others to identify with and help you. Just remember to be prudent about it.

SELF-REFLECTION TIME

- ◎ As a leader, when and how have you shown vulnerability?

- ◎ Do you find it difficult to be vulnerable with those you lead? If so, why do you think this is?

"I think the leader today has to demonstrate both transparency and vulnerability, and with that comes truthfulness and humility."

– Howard Schultz

CHAPTER 24

Lead with Open Mindedness

If you have an open mind, you can listen to mentors or read their words and learn from many and varied bodies of knowledge. Wisely chosen mentors can expose you to what they have learned from experiences that you would never have.

I have many mentors, and it may surprise you to know that most of them I have never even met face to face. With today's technology and the Internet, it's easier now than ever to be mentored by some inspiring and incredible people who are far, far away. You can follow their personal social media accounts, listen to their podcasts, watch their videos on YouTube or read their books. You don't necessarily have to have a personal relationship with a mentor or a coach to learn from them. Like me, they can be virtual mentors!

One such person I've never met but have regarded as a mentor is George Raveling. Born in 1937, George played basketball at Villanova University and was the head coach at Washington State University, the University of Iowa and the University of Southern California. He has also been Nike's global basketball sports marketing director since he retired from coaching in 1994.

A few years ago, I listened to an interview with George, who was 79 years old at the time. He spoke about the importance of moving with the times, adapting and staying open-minded. I found it a fascinating conversation. Here was a man who had achieved much success in his career but showed no signs of slowing down or resting on his laurels. This had a positive impact on me, not only as a leader, but as a human being. It reaffirmed the value of being open-minded.

A few years later, George wrote in a newsletter: "At 82, I am still a work in progress. I am on a daily self-discovery journey to find myself, the real me. I have come to learn that in life, things do not happen to you; they happen for you, and it is not just what happens but how you react to it that matters. The moment we stop exploring and discovering who we are is the moment we die while still being alive." He added, "At 82, I, too, am still learning, unlearning, relearning, and mastering." Wow! Isn't that inspirational? By keeping an open mind and a hungry heart, George is still as relevant and sought after as he was over 40 years ago.

Another example of staying open-minded and relevant is John Maxwell, a best-selling author on the subject of leadership. In a podcast recorded when he was 72, John spoke about the importance of staying open-minded. He stressed the value of being willing to learn from anyone, no matter who they are, what their status is, or what they have achieved in life. Some of life's greatest insights can come from some of the least likely sources.

Open-minded leaders, like George and John, have a thirst for learning, even after being at the top of their games for decades. Their learning journey never stops. No matter how old you are, maintain a student-like mindset toward life and learning. And as George suggested, sometimes the best open-minded learning is unlearning.

Generally speaking, open-minded leaders—and people—are more tolerant and approachable, partly because they are willing to listen to what others have to say without passing judgment. They make the effort to see from another person's point of view. Because they are evenhanded, they don't care as much about being right as they care about understanding.

Being open-minded and willing to learn from others is a choice. Here's another bit of wisdom from George, who has the advantage one gains from being a leader and knowing many people in many places: "No two people think the same way because no two people have lived the same lives. Because our thinking limits us, we need to listen to others to open up our minds."

At the opposite end of the spectrum is being closed minded. Closed-minded leaders are stuck in their own beliefs and have an attitude of "This is what I think, and I'm not going to change." Unfortunately, this kind of mindset stunts growth and traps people in the world of yesterday. Recognize that dynamics are always changing. You don't want to be like the people who told Henry Ford that nothing could replace the horse.

It's you who gets to choose. You can hold yourself back by staying inside your own box, believing you already have all the answers and know everything—or you can commit to not only being more open to new knowledge but also to new challenges and experiences.

Steve Jobs did not get where he was by believing he knew more than his employees. He wisely noted, "It doesn't make sense to hire smart people and then tell them what to do. We hire smart people so they can tell us what to do."

Stay open-minded and learn from others. Surround yourself with people who can help you learn, grow and expand your goals.

SELF-REFLECTION TIME

- ◎ As a leader, would you describe yourself as open-minded? If so, provide some examples.
- ◎ In what ways do you think being more open-minded could make you a better leader?

"In order to grow we must be open to new ideas, new ways of doing things and new ways of thinking."

– George Raveling

CHAPTER 25

Lead with Honesty

W hen you first step into a leadership role, you might as well assume that people don't completely trust you. And why should they? Trust must be earned.

Being an honest leader is not always easy. First, you need to be honest with yourself. That means admitting that you have weaknesses and that you need to make changes. Second, you need to be honest with those you lead. Having the tough conversations within the team can be quite challenging. The truth can be painful, but it is the only way to change people and situations for the better. As a leader, you have to be willing to have the face-to-face honest but uncomfortable conversations.

Phil Neville played for Manchester United and held coaching roles at clubs such as Everton, Valencia, and Inter Miami. He also managed the Lionesses (England's women's team). When asked what he found important in a coach when he was still a player, Phil cited honesty as imperative. He added that on the [rare] occasions he was dropped from the starting line-up, he far preferred that a coach be honest, even brutally honest, in delivering the bad news.

Neville, who also played for England 59 times, simply wanted to know where he stood. Having played under the leadership of Sir Alex Ferguson at Manchester United and then David Moyes at Everton, he was fortunate to always know that, like it or not, he would get honest feedback from both.

Neville also noted that the players who couldn't handle criticism never seemed to improve or grow. They couldn't be honest with themselves, so as a result, many of them found themselves looking for other teams. Think about that. As a leader, don't you want to know who can handle the truth and learn from it?

From the time I was playing youth sports through my professional years, the people in leadership positions I respected most were the ones who were tough but fair. They were the ones who told me the whole truth. The message may have stung at the time, but their honesty told me that they cared about me. I carry their lessons today. They were the people who greatly and positively influenced my relationships, my career and my life. They taught me how to lead myself as well as others forthrightly.

Leaders who want respect and trust from their followers must model integrity. As with the leaders who influenced me, their honesty sets the example that inspires their people to likewise deal with others frankly. In his book *What It Takes to Be #1*, Vince Lombardi Jr., son of the legendary Green Bay Packers coach Vince Lombardi Sr., writes that his father frequently reminded folks that "to be successful you've got to be honest with yourself." People sense when others, especially leaders, are less than forthright. As a result, trust is lost.

Effective leaders keep everyone abreast of what is going on within the organization or team—good and bad. Leaders who cover all sides are much more respected than leaders who keep to themselves information that should be communicated. In successful organizations and teams, you will find a more open and honest culture. When team members speak more freely, issues can be dealt with and new and creative solutions can advance the team's goals.

In fact, a recent worldwide study of Gen Y and Gen Z conducted by research and consulting firm Millennial Branding and HR services and staffing company Randstad revealed that just over half of these populations believe that honesty is the single most important quality for good leaders.

As a leader, you can have the best vision or strategy, but your people will not buy into it if they don't trust you. However, when they know you are shooting straight with them, they will trust you implicitly and will look up to you as a person who is worth following. You will also further inspire them to follow their own path of honesty.

Despite the fact that tough situations can arise from being an honest leader, the benefits significantly outweigh the drawbacks. The bottom line is that, whatever the leadership structure may be—sports teams, corporations or symphony orchestras—people want to follow leaders they can rely on to be honest. Be that person for your people. You will be a more satisfied leader, your team will respect you, and your organization will be built on a stronger and more long-lasting foundation.

Honesty really is the best policy.

SELF-REFLECTION TIME

- ◎ As a leader, do you find it difficult at times to give honest feedback? Why?
- ◎ When giving feedback, especially bad news, are you completely honest?

"To be successful,
you've got to be honest with yourself."

– Vince Lombardi Jr.

CHAPTER 26

Lead with Self-Confidence

If you were to create your own list of the traits of a great leader, I'd bet that self-confidence would be near the top. People don't follow leaders who lack confidence. You can be the most competent and experienced individual in your field, but if you lack the confidence to back it up, you will be unable to lead successfully. Conversely, if you have self-confidence but don't have the competence to back it up, people will see through your charade.

Retired Chicago Bulls and LA Lakers head coach Phil Jackson once said, "I think the most important thing about coaching is that you have to have a sense of confidence about what you're doing. You have to be a salesman and you have to get your players, particularly your team leaders, to believe in what you're trying to accomplish on the basketball floor." Throughout his coaching career, Jackson was successful in achieving these goals in grand style.

In a 2016 study conducted at the University of Texas at San Antonio, researchers determined that confidence is key to a creative and successful leader. According to the study, leadership isn't only about motivating people, but also about developing new ideas and selling them. Not surprising. Furthermore, confident people get ahead of the game. Because of the way they prepare and present themselves, they are able to sell their views and proposals in such a way that they become the norm.

Over the years, I have met leaders from diverse fields. What stands out is that those who have been the most successful are those who possess a healthy amount of confidence. They are, in fact, confident enough to show vulnerability, admit their shortcomings and make adjustments.

Moreover, they value the creative insights gained from involving their people in decision making. And they are secure enough in the people they have chosen for their team that they don't feel the need to micromanage. Consequently, their people are devoted to the organization, their own self-confidence grows and they are motivated to realize their potential.

During my days living in South Africa, I had the opportunity to work with the former captain of the South African cricket team, Graeme Smith. Even though Graeme was only 19 years of age at the time, it struck me just how confident and mature he already was. Of course, back then he wasn't yet captaining or playing for his country, but it was obvious that he was destined to have a great career. Graeme exuded healthy confidence, and that really left an impression on me. I discovered while working with him that he had great leadership skills having captained his school and provincial junior teams. Graeme went on to become South Africa's youngest ever national captain at the age of 22.

Effective leadership is about having the confidence and courage to make the hard decisions and to call out poor effort or performance and poor behavior or standards. If a leader is not willing to assume these tasks, then not only will the culture become toxic, but more importantly, the people within the organization will lose trust and respect in the leader. And there are more consequences. Team members may fail to perform and, further, may leave the leader, literally or figuratively, without a work force. Or they may make decisions on their own. Or they may just find a way to get the leader replaced.

Leaders with self-confidence deal immediately and directly with problems and conflicts, rather than side-step, ignore or pass the problems to others. Your people are looking to you, the leader, to go first, to be the first to walk into the line of fire and to face challenges or adversities with courage and confidence. This is how respect and trust are earned.

Think optimistically and positively about the future. Be willing to take calculated and morally correct risks to achieve your personal and professional goals. If a leader lacks confidence, their people will not feel secure and safe.

So, what if confidence is something you lack? The good news is that confidence is something that can be worked on and improved. Engage in simple practices like self-reflecting in a positive way and recognizing your strengths. Celebrate your small wins on a daily basis and spend some time recognizing and reconnecting with your strongest talents as ways to stay focused on your strengths.

Another way to build your confidence is to surround yourself with positive people and confident leaders you can learn and grow from. Take note of how they interact with others, how they present themselves (body language, eye contact, clothing, etc.), how they talk, and how they go about their day.

Leadership is about having the confidence to make decisions. If the person in charge is afraid to commit to decisions, all of the communication and empowerment in the world won't make a difference.

Self-confidence is a mindset, and it's you who gets to choose. Without it, it's almost impossible to achieve your goals and make the difference you have in mind. If you build it in yourself, exemplify it for others, and foster it in your team, all of you will reap the rewards.

SELF-REFLECTION TIME

- ◎ Would you describe yourself as a confident leader?

- ◎ Who are some leaders you know who exude confidence? How do they display it?

"I think the most important thing about coaching is that you have to have a sense of confidence about what you are doing."

– Phil Jackson

CHAPTER 27

Lead with Collaboration

L eaders who build their vision with collaboration are most likely to achieve long-term success. It can be no surprise that people who work well together and trust each other eventually succeed together.

November 2, 2016, is a night I'll never forget. If you are Chicago Cubs baseball fan, you will recognize the date. I was in the Windy City (Chicago) attending a leaders conference on the night of the World Series final game 7. Let me add that it was the night I paid the most for a rideshare ride just a few blocks from my hotel to a meeting I was attending!

Facing the unmatched pressure of 108 years without a World Series win (the longest in the history of a professional sports team of this stature), Joe Maddon's Chicago Cubs overcame adversity and an emotional rollercoaster to claim victory. After more than a century of pain, the Cubs had finally won the World Series, defeating the Cleveland Indians 8-7 in a 10-inning cliffhanger. It was also the same week that the mighty All Blacks rugby team was in Chicago to play Ireland, who stamped their names into the history books by dispatching New Zealand 40-29 for their first win over the All Blacks in 111 years! Talk about a historic week in sports history!

Back to Joe Maddon and the Cubs. How did they finally pull off this momentous victory? Maddon said that it ultimately came down to 3 values: empowerment, trust, and collaboration. Maddon believes that a leader's greatest responsibility is to create a positive environment, one that promotes growth and success. To do that, he explained, collaboration is the secret sauce as he works to personally connect with his staff and players. By getting to know the people he works with, he is able to build relationships that enable a candid exchange of information. It is personal connections between individuals that create the kind of trust that's necessary for high-performing teams. Maddon's goal is staff-wide collaboration: everyone in the building working as one, sharing ideas and supporting one another.

Why do we sometimes see a group of star individuals on a sports team who just never live up to expectations? The truth is that even when many of the right elements exist, if the team doesn't share a vision and work toward it collaboratively, it will be difficult for them to make progress.

One of the most incredible sporting achievements ever is Leicester City winning the English premiership title back in 2016 under Claudio Ranieri. For more than 30 years, the same five football teams had completely dominated the English Premier League due to money, influence and support behind each of these global clubs. Leicester City had a hideous 5,000-1 odds to win the Premier League Title on the opening day of that season. To put it into perspective, the odds were better for President Obama playing cricket for England and Elvis Presley still being alive in Memphis than for Leicester City winning the premiership. However, under Claudio Ranieri's management and leadership skills, the impossible was achieved. His secret sauce, as with Joe Maddon, was getting to know each player, recognizing each one's strengths and weaknesses and using them wisely. By creating a team that played as one, Ranieri was able to get the best from everyone. The unity was reflected in the attitude and collaboration of the players themselves who were able to put their individual wants and needs aside for the sake of the team.

Another example of success through collaboration was created by Leeds United Football Club and their manager, Marcelo Bielsa. The Australian company Gain Line Analytics has developed a unique metric, the Team Work Index (TWI®), that measures the quantity and intensity of linkages within a team. The higher the number, the more cohesive the team on the Team Work Index, the more unified the team is and the more likely it is to enjoy sustained on-field success and off-field stability. In their successful promotion to the Premier League in 2020, Leeds United scored the highest on this index. It was evident that Marcelo Bielsa had fostered a culture of cohesion and collaboration among his players.

Moreover, where there is collaboration, there is usually good chemistry. With collaboration and chemistry, great things happen. Teams that collaborate well have a different vibe and energy about them. It almost always looks like they are having fun while putting in the hard work that's required. In fact, just a few days after the season concluded, I was in Ibiza, Spain, where the Leeds players and their partners were staying at my hotel. You'd think that after a full season of practically living together, these players would want a break from each other! No. There they were, not only teammates but best mates!

In successful organizations and teams, you'll find a group of people who have come together, respect each other's differences, and collaborate well. You will find a certain energy and good chemistry among them. They might not agree all the time, but they have a mutual understanding that it is *not about who is right, but about what is right for the greater good* of the team and its vision. The *who is right* approach is usually driven by ego and insecurities, whereas *what is right* is driven by values, open-mindedness and collaboration.

Organizations and teams that pay attention to collaboration are comprised of people who are absent of ego or personal agenda. They all bring different expertise, experiences, knowledge and perspectives to the table. They stay open-mined, listen well and have an ability to come together and brainstorm to find solutions and implement them.

The purpose of collaborative leadership is to value the ideas and input from team members, giving everyone a chance to voice their opinion and contribute. According to *Harvard Business Review*, good leaders regularly seek out diverse opinions and ideas among team members. As a result, team members feel more engaged and trusted and are more likely to take ownership of their work.

Leaders who drive collaboration within their organization and actively listen to the ideas and opinions of their people allow them to build more confidence and more cohesiveness. Their people speak up and share their thoughts without the fear of consequences. The result is a group who trust each other, work well together and, in fact, enjoy it.

As American author, political activist and lecturer Helen Keller once said, "Alone we can do so little; together we can do so much."

SELF-REFLECTION TIME

- ◎ What are some of the biggest obstacles to getting a team to collaborate?

- ◎ As a leader, how best do you get a team to collaborate well?

"What matters most is getting the best out of the squad you have. It's all about collaboration and putting in the work."

– Claudio Ranieri

CHAPTER 28

Lead with Positivity

If you want to lead from a place of positive energy, you must first create that energy. It comes from within you. Before you can influence and inspire others, you must first lead and inspire yourself.

Great leaders know that positivity and energy are contagious, and both result in a heightened level of motivation and enthusiasm. It is the leader's job to infect each member of their team with enthusiasm toward the realization of the team's goals. I've always thought of leaders as a kind of thermostat. They are the ones who ultimately control the temperature—and passion— in the room.

The great NFL football coach Don Shula once noted, "My responsibility is leadership, and the minute I get negative, that is going to have an influence on my team." What Shula understood well was that, whether consciously or not, the attitude and energy you bring are contagious. Be self-aware.

One of the most successful rugby coaches ever, Eddie Jones, has coached, among others, the national teams of Australia, England and Japan. He believes that as a coach you have to be cognizant of what you say, because you are saying something either positive or negative: There is no neutral. Your words are either empowering people or hurting them. Choose to empower.

In my first book, *7 Keys to Being a Great Coach*, one of the seven keys is Energy. The Energy chapter highlights the importance of keeping a great energy as a coach or leader because it sets the tone. The truth is that no one wants to be led by, or be anywhere around, someone who is constantly negative, sarcastic, pessimistic or critical. Neither does anyone want to be around an energy vampire who sucks the life out of you. Maybe you can relate if you have had to spend time around such a person.

After their extremely successful campaign at the 2018 World Soccer Cup in Russia, a reporter asked a staff member on the England football team what had made manager Gareth Southgate successful during England's run to the semi-finals. He replied, "Simple. Gareth is grounded, with the confidence of a man with a plan and trust in his team. He empowers others, demonstrates emotional intelligence, and genuinely cares for his staff and players. He also stays extremely positive even when things aren't going well." Gareth also led England to the finals in the 2020 Euro Cup.

What positive leaders understand better than others is that there is always something great to be found in every day. Positive leaders don't believe in "bad days"; they believe in learning and growing days. Even if they have received unfavorable news, they look for the silver lining in every dark cloud.

In my years of working closely with all kinds of teams, I have observed that the ones that are led by upbeat leaders are more likely to go above and beyond. Their members feel privileged and proud to belong to the organization or team they are with.

Pat Summit was the winningest college basketball coach (male or female) of her time. She was known as an intense and passionate leader who was endlessly committed to bringing out the best in her players. Summit always brought a high level of energy, and she demanded it from her players every single day. She took the time to recognize the everyday positives in her players' behaviors and rewarded the small wins. Although she could be tough on them, her players adored her. Over her illustrious coaching career in college basketball, she repeatedly demonstrated that small successes over time add up to big wins.

Especially in the sports world, sometimes coaches who are seen as positive can be mistaken as soft. Being a positive coach or leader doesn't mean that you are always the happy smiley one who just high fives everyone and hands out compliments. Like Pat Summit, you can be demanding, but you can remain positive and encouraging. Remember that constructive criticism isn't being negative: It's being helpful; it builds people up. It's a necessity for progress—and in the end, that's a positive.

Chances are that if you don't get this, you are tearing down your team members and limiting team potential. Employing constructive criticism will yield both short-term and long-term success.

When you lead with high standards and positivity, you inspire and motivate others to go far and above what is expected. Great leaders and coaches avoid providing too much criticism. Bill Walsh, the legendary football coach once said, "People thrive on positive reinforcement. They can take only a certain amount of criticism, and you may lose them altogether if you criticize them in a personal way—you can make a point without being personal. Don't insult or belittle your people. Instead of getting more out of them, you will get less."

When challenges arise (and there is never a shortage), positive leaders are skilled at finding solutions. They don't waste valuable time and energy complaining, moaning, or passing the buck. They go straight into finding-solutions mode.

In leadership, we find that the road to achievement and success is at times lined with obstacles, challenges and the unexpected. When you maintain a positive perspective, these kinds of challenges aren't overwhelming. You see them as predictable parts of the journey. Upbeat leaders rebound more quickly than those who are negative. After a failure or setback, they dust themselves off and carry on.

Energy, as I've said, is contagious, so It's easy to see how negative and pessimistic leaders create toxic atmospheres that their team will pick up and respond to. Walk into an organization where the energy is low and the attitudes are poor, and you will find that it stems from poor leadership.

Positive leaders create cultures and environments where growth and opportunity flourish. It's this kind of atmosphere that inspires excellence and success.

SELF-REFLECTION TIME

- ◉ Describe some ways you see yourself as a positive leader.

- ◉ As a leader, how do you remain positive in times of difficulty or adversity?

"My responsibility is leadership, and the minute I get negative, that is going to have an influence on my team."

– Don Shula

CHAPTER 29

Lead with Courage

C ourage, Aristotle wrote, is the virtue that makes the others possible. It is a characteristic typical in great leaders.

If you are the person in charge, you must be willing to deal with a wide variety of challenging tasks, and it will take courage. You will face complex dilemmas that have no good options, only poor ones and other poor ones, bad ones and other bad ones. It can be lonely. As Mahatma Gandhi said, "It's easy to stand in the crowd, but it takes courage to stand alone."

Sometimes things run smoothly. You feel like whistling. Then out of the blue tough decisions drop in your lap like a ton of bricks, and it's hard to whistle. It's up to you to make the calls because, as the sign on Harry President Truman's desk noted, you are where the buck stops.

Jill Ellis, the former United States women's soccer coach is the first coach in history to have back-to-back wins in the women's world cup. Jill knows about making tough calls, and she believes that courage is part of the job. "I believe it takes courage to be a great leader. You have got to be willing to make the tough calls and sometimes be the unpopular one. I think leading is also about having a very clear sense of your own identity, of your values, and of what you want to achieve."

Among the tough tasks, as we have noted, are uncomfortable conversations. Leaders can struggle with them, and that's only natural. They are difficult, and it's hard to gauge how well or poorly the recipients will respond. Nonetheless, you must gut it up. In her book *Dare to Lead*, best-selling author Brené Brown advises leaders to choose courage over comfort.

In fact, courage can determine whether leaders have the influence they need over those they lead. If you have people, whatever their position in the organization, who are choosing to ignore them or choosing to display poor attitudes, they must be dealt with. These little talks can be difficult if, for example, the person plays a particularly important role on the team. They can be awkward if you and the other person have an especially close relationship. No matter. The integrity of the organization is of highest importance.

There are several positive outcomes from handling these conversations properly. Other team members will know that everybody will be held accountable and nobody gets a pass. They will think twice before acting irresponsibly themselves, and they will be more willing to hold each other responsible. Consequently, you will have to deal with fewer problems in the future. People inside and outside your organization will admire your courage. And you will have an organization, and team members, to be proud of.

Part of being the one in charge is delegating. Choosing the right person for a given job requires getting to know them. It's a process that involves letting them get to know you, too. You learn each other's strengths and weaknesses. You make a real connection. You see how they can be of most help within the organization, and they feel gratified that you see this and trust them to live up to your opinion of them.

Leaders need to be steadfast in their beliefs, values and standards. When they are not willing to do this, they eventually end up with a distrustful, disruptive and toxic culture. If they are not willing to stand up and take action, the result is anarchy.

Whether you make the best decision ever or make one that keeps you up at night, be ready for criticism. Be ready to own up to your bad call—even if your bad call was putting the wrong person in the position to make their bad call. It's part of the job of sitting in your chair.

Courageous leaders are able to push through prickly situations. They are willing to make difficult decisions and do not back down when things get tough.

Leadership requires a certain kind of person who will speak when the pressure is on to stay silent. NBA coach Doc Rivers of the LA Clippers often talks about the importance of having courage as a coach. He believes that you just aren't going to please everyone all the time. Steve Jobs noted, "If you want to make everyone happy, don't be a leader; go sell ice cream." So true!

To be a leader of impact, one of the first things you have to do is decide that you are going to be a courageous leader, no matter what. You have to be willing to go through the fire, climb over obstacles, and do what's maybe not pleasant. You are not always going to win the popularity contest.

Great leaders want to take their people to new and loftier goals. Getting there requires courage, starting at the top. If they aren't willing to show courage, then no one else in the organization will either. The best news of all is that courage can be learned—by the leader and by the members of the team. Think of it as a muscle that must be strengthened day by day, choice by choice. Exercise it.

SELF-REFLECTION TIME

- As a leader, how courageous are you in making the bigger decisions and having the tougher conversations?

- What is an example of a recent conversation you had to have that felt uncomfortable? Were you happy with the way you conducted it?

"The ultimate measure of a man is not where he stands in moments of comfort, but where he stands in times of challenge and controversy."

– Martin Luther King Jr.

CHAPTER 30

Lead with Connection

In leadership, as in life, potential to achieve goals depends on how well the person in charge and those who look to them for direction develop strong and trusting relationships.

Awhile back I had a conversation with the owner of a flourishing real estate company in Fort Lauderdale, Florida. I asked him what he attributed his long-term success to. His enthusiastic reply: "Everything in leadership involves developing trusting relationships. You can't forget that your own success as well as theirs depends on how you connect with your people and your network and the quality of the relationships you build over time." He stressed that using your interpersonal skills and making an emotional connection are fundamental to driving loyalty. Building trust and acceptance brings your people closer to you, to each other and to the organization's goals." Connections create a shared "we got this" mindset.

Christian Horner, team principal at Red Bull Formula 1, is someone who understands the importance of building connections and having good interpersonal skills, especially in a high-pressure environment. In an interview he said, "It's all about people. It's about working with people. It's about having the ability to engage with people at any level, whether it's a sponsor or a truck driver. It's having the ability to be approachable."

From my coaching days working with Olympic athletes and professional sports teams, I learned that it wasn't my knowledge, experience or skills that would help me succeed most. While those are all requirements, what made the difference was that I connected well with those I was around. In my book *7 Keys to Being a Great Coach* one of those 7 keys is Interpersonal Skills, the ability to connect and get along with others. I discovered that the more connected and invested I became in others, the more connection they felt with me. This, I believe, was a major factor in my ultimately working with some of the world's best performers and leading organizations.

Manager and head coach of Leicester City Football Club Brendan Rodgers says that high performing coaches and leaders take genuine interest in the individual. Rodgers wants to get to know the person behind the player. He wants to know their backgrounds, their families, their interests, and what makes them tick.

Rodgers sees this as an important step in building a strong professional relationship and a level of mutual trust. He believes that a leader or coach who demonstrates a genuine interest in their people builds a stronger connection and shows each person that they care. Leaders who are connected use compassion, empathy and trust to build influence with their people. They understand that when they have a stronger connection, and its members are likely to follow them and be more loyal.

The most effective working environments are those where the employees and team members feel like family. Of course, just as in a family, there will be disagreements and issues that arise from time to time. But because of the close relationships and connections between team members, they are able to resolve problems more quickly and move on. In these cultures, there is a high level of trust and togetherness.

So, how can leaders become more connected? First, remember that attitudes start at the top and work down. A leader must create an environment that encourages and nurtures connections. Second, connections are made when people spend some non-working time together. So, it's important for the leader to carve out time for the leader and team members to spend some less structured time together. This is team building.

When it comes to connecting with those you lead or coach, I love what Ben Ryan, the Rio Olympic gold medal winning coach with the Fiji rugby 7s squad, shared with me. "If you really want to build solid connections with those you coach or work alongside, then what counts is how well you know each other. Get below the transactional stuff and chat about what else they are about. What drives them, who inspired them, what does their best version of themselves look like—it all can only help to bind your relationship. So, when the turbulent times come (and they always do), your connections stay tight and together. It's two-way, too. Let your people know about you. Be open, be transparent. Show more of yourself to them so it's a reciprocal relationship."

In a conversation I had with an Australian AFL coach, he shared that his organization had what he called a "speed dating" session every few weeks for everyone in the building—including players, office staff, food and beverage workers, security, etc. The protocol was that everyone spent 5 minutes with each other asking and answering questions about one another. He explained that after these sessions, there was more of a connection and chemistry among the individuals and the groups. He believed that this was a major contributing factor to building a healthier and more enjoyable environment. He successfully created a culture where people knew each other personally and got along like a family.

Remember that as the leader, you are *the* greatest example, *the* role model for your people. If you aren't making the effort to foster connections and relationships, your team probably won't either. Sitting in your office with the door shut or keeping your distance from your people make you a mushroom; people keep you in the dark and give you only the manure they want you to have. You need to see the whole picture. Tim Draper, founder of Draper Fisher Jurvetson, says, "I like to wander around randomly and connect with my team members, ask them what they're doing, and how they're doing." His wisdom created a venture capital firm with estimated assets of $5 billion. Making your team members feel valued has its rewards.

When you establish connections with your team members on a personal level, they will feel that you genuinely care about them, understand their point of view and value their contributions. Your well earned results: Collaboration and trust increase, and productivity flourishes.

SELF-REFLECTION TIME

- ◎ What are examples of how you connect with those you lead?
- ◎ In what ways do you feel you could build even better connections within your organization or team?

"If you really want to build solid connections with those you coach or work alongside, then what counts is how well you know each other."

– Ben Ryan

CHAPTER 31

Lead with Growth Mindedness

L ook behind the walls of any successful organization or team and you will most likely find a positive and growth-minded leader. What we know about leadership is that the beliefs, values and mindsets of leaders rub off on their people. Without a forward-thinking leader, an organization is locked into today.

The term "growth mindset" is the brainchild of Dr. Carol Dweck, an author and Stanford researcher who has spent many years studying human behavior and performance. She believes that organizations fall into two mindsets: fixed and growth. Furthermore, which one an organization aligns with today ultimately shapes its future.

Let's define what growth minded versus fixed minded leadership looks like. Growth minded organizations promote learning, developing and being unafraid to make mistakes. Such organizations create a safe environment that allows people to expand their skills and talents. The atmosphere nurtures creative thinking that can boost the organization to the next level.

Growth-minded leaders focus more on processes than on outcomes. With this perspective, their team members believe that mistakes allow them to learn so they can do it better the next time. In fact, growth-minded people see mistakes and failures as the best teachers and as pathways to eventual success.

On the other hand, there is the fixed mindset. Not having a growth-minded outlook holds many leaders back from achieving their greatest potential. They are not interested in promoting learning. They fear trying something new that might fail. They don't realize that failures offer big opportunities—opportunities that may not pass their way again—to learn, grow and succeed in ways they can't possibly foresee. They operate with the belief that people are who they are and that abilities and talents are set and cannot be developed.

Moreover, fixed-minded leaders avoid change due to, among other things, fear of getting uncomfortable or fear of looking incompetent in front of others. They create a culture where team members become afraid to even share ideas, let alone take risks or innovate. The team becomes a group of unmotivated and uncommitted individuals.

Leaders with a fixed mindset are a detriment to their people and to their organization. Those who shrink from calculated risk and real possibilities eventually stagnate and wither away. The real tragedy occurs when they are allowed to hang around the organization and relegate everyone to the world of the dial phone.

In his book *Good to Great,* Jim Collins discusses his study of companies that made the leap to greatness. One factor was their curious, self-effacing leaders who asked the tough questions and confronted the tough issues. They nurtured the concept of new ideas and new possibilities in their people.

In great cultures you will find leaders who are sufficiently secure in themselves to allow other voices to be heard. They want their team members, too, to be sufficiently secure in themselves, and in the organization's culture, to offer divergent opinions. Assurance from their leaders that team members' suggestions will be seriously considered drives optimal outcomes.

Awhile into my journey as a coach, I realized that something wasn't working. I had to face the fact that if I continued to coach the way I had been coached earlier in my life, I would soon become irrelevant or even unemployed! Growing up in South Africa, I was brought up with a very authoritarian style of leadership. However, generations and attitudes change, and I had to unlearn, relearn and keep evolving to stay relevant. You are not obligated to coach (or lead) the way you once were or the way you have been doing it. A fixed mindset will keep you trapped where you are.

Today's modern leaders are not stuck in their old ways of doing things. They ask, "How can we do things better?" They promote healthy learning environments by continually investing in their people and looking for new ways to create opportunities.

For leaders—and others—with a fixed mindset the good news is that they can learn to think with a growth mindset. Our brain is elastic, not cast in concrete. We can unlearn fixed, obstructive thinking and replace it with a growth, constructive mindset.

Kevin Rutherford, CEO of Nuun, a wellness company that has been named a top company to work for by *Outside Magazine* for four years in a row, believes, "Leadership is about having a growth mindset. You can never stop learning and growing if you want to sustain as the team's leader. So, in effect, it's not a destination, as you always need to evolve to be a leader."

SELF-REFLECTION TIME

- ◎ As a leader, would you describe yourself as growth or fixed minded? Why?

- ◎ How do you approach learning new things and learning from others?

"You're in charge of your mind. You can help it grow by using it in the right way."

– Carol Dweck

CHAPTER 32

Lead with Questions

One of the starter questions leaders should ask themselves is, Am I supplying solutions to problems without asking my people for their input? Great leaders don't assume they know everything. They ask their people questions and then pay attention to their answers. In addition, they encourage their people to ask questions, which they pay attention to as well.

I've been an all-in sports fan since I was a kid. In fact, I can watch almost any sport. I'm attracted not just by the competition, but also by the different styles of the coaches. Most intriguing is watching the different ways coaches communicate and motivate. Do they tell their people how and what to think, or do they teach them to think on their own and to ask their own questions?

One sport that I've always loved is Formula 1 motor racing. I especially loved the days of the legendary Brazilian driver Ayrton Senna and the German 7-time world champion Michael Schumacher. One of the most dominant teams currently is the Mercedes Petronas F1 team under the leadership of team principal Toto Wolff. At the time of this writing, they have won both the drivers' and the constructors' (manufacturers') championships 2014-2020.

It's one thing to have a successful season in a sport, but it's another to maintain dominance over a period of years. Especially when you are at the top, the competition is always trying to chase you down. Wolff believes that in order to stay at the front of the pack, it's important that he is not the only one talking. He wants to ask questions—and get the team members to ask questions—that keep everyone evolving, innovating and improving.

Wolff encourages his staff—well over 1900 employees—to voice their opinions because he believes that hearing them is important for his own development, as well as everyone else's. After difficult races where the team might not have performed to expectations, Wolff wants his people to question what they did right and wrong so they can learn and grow.

The interesting thing is that Wolff doesn't come from a traditional motorsports background, but from a financial investment background where asking questions was the norm. He transferred this philosophy to sport and ascribes the team's success to "permanent skepticism" about what they are currently doing and the "relentless pursuit of excellence." It is these principles that propelled both his team and his main driver, Lewis Hamilton, to their seventh world title in 2020.

Great leaders, like Wolff, understand the power in asking questions rather than always providing their own (only one person's) solutions. Wolff believes that when you provide people with more questions than answers, they will begin to tackle solving those problems themselves rather than trying to involve you every time. He also believes that by teaching people to ask their own questions, you are giving them the opportunity to build their own decision making muscles and learn to solve problems on their own.

Another of Wolff's stand-up practices is having what he terms a "no blame" culture. When something goes wrong, instead of blaming a person, he blames the problem. He believes that when there is a blame culture, no one wins. The time wasted pointing fingers can be more productively spent finding solutions. This is their "see it, say it, fix it" mantra, which Wolff says is another factor in their progress. It encourages everybody in the organization to speak up, question things and point out shortcomings and deficits.

The most important lesson we can take from Toto Wolff and the Mercedes Petronas F1 team is not how to race cars, but instead how to implement the approach of thinking about how things are done now, asking how they could be done better and finding solutions.

SELF-REFLECTION TIME

- ◎ As a leader, what is the area where you are strongest in asking questions?

- ◎ What area should you work on next?

"I think today you can't be an effective leader if you're not willing to be open-minded."

– Toto Wolff

CHAPTER 33

Lead with Commitment

W hen asked about commitment, former NBA coach and president of the Miami Heat basketball team Pat Riley leaves no doubt. "There are only two options regarding commitment. You're either in or out. There's no such thing as a life in between."

Without commitment, success isn't possible. If the leader isn't committed, then who will be? You can't expect your people to be committed and to be giving their best if you are not. Great leaders model the commitment they wish to see in their team. Commitment is a kind of glue in an organization. It provides a common goal, focus and camaraderie—all essential to any organization or team's success and longevity.

Lack of commitment in leadership comes in many forms. A few months ago, I was having dinner with a good friend who is the CEO of a highly successful company based near my home in West Palm Beach, Florida. He told me about an employee in his company who was excellent at making sales. Unfortunately, he wasn't a good team player. He sometimes said one thing but did another. He was poor in communication and time management, and his fellow team members felt he couldn't be trusted. His team believed he was not committed or reliable enough to stay. Even his enviable productivity couldn't overcome his lack of big-picture commitment to the team, and he was gone.

When you are in a job you don't enjoy, you will most likely find it hard to stay motivated and committed for the long run. But when you are passionate about what you do, it's easier to feel inspired and stay committed: Seek jobs or a career field that you love; don't just chase money, a mistake many make.

Real commitment comes from a deeper place. Committed leaders have a greater purpose to what they do, and it's through this purpose that they are able to stay in it—and committed—into the future. Coach and hall of famer Sue Enquist holds more national championships than anyone in the history of college softball. In 2006, Enquist, who concluded her storied 27-year career as head coach of the UCLA Bruins and as the winningest softball coach among all active coaches, agrees. "It's simple. Whether you're a leader or team member, there is no in-between in commitment. You cannot be kind of committed. You're either all in or you're not. On good days and bad days, be committed."

So, what does a committed leader look like? If you are a committed leader, you show up with enthusiasm and a strong desire to lead your people. You are willing to give more than what's been asked of you. You are willing to stand firm through the very worst of times and still be there fighting for the greater cause. You are there for your team members through the most difficult challenges. You are able to take full responsibility and ownership even for something done by someone of lower rank in your organization because, of course, the buck stops with you. Commitment is having the discipline to do what you said you'd do long after the motivation has worn off.

On a team level, if you are a committed leader, you do what's best for the team. You find solutions. You are usually very good at making decisions, but you aren't afraid to bring in other voices for information and insight. You recognize outstanding efforts and performances from your team and each member. You play the role of not only the leader, but also the mentor and coach. You build an environment and culture that fosters growth and encourages your people to do their best work. You know that true success means helping others be successful and that getting ahead means helping others get ahead.

Whew! Commitment is not for the faint of heart. For a great leader, it's a requirement.

One of my favorite quotes comes courtesy of racing car legend Mario Andretti. "Desire is the key to motivation, but it's determination and commitment to an unrelenting pursuit of your goal—a commitment to excellence—that will enable you to attain the success you seek."

SELF-REFLECTION TIME

- ◎ What does a committed leader look like to you? Can you provide some examples?

- ◎ In terms of leadership, what are the areas that you feel you could be more committed in?

"There are only two options regarding commitment. You're either in or out. There's no such thing as a life in between."

– Pat Riley

CHAPTER 34

Lead with Humility

The people I most admire are those who have been extraordinarily successful but remained grounded and humble. There are many personalities in the sports world who live these admirable traits. English football player David Beckham, Spanish tennis champion Rafael Nadal and multiple Olympic gold medal gymnast Simone Biles immediately come to mind. Away from sports, the German chancellor Angela Merkel, the late South African president Nelson Mandela and the billionaire businesswomen who founded Spanx, Sara Blakely. All of these people maintained a sense of humility no matter what heights they reached in their chosen fields.

One such person who led his team with humility was the legendary UCLA basketball coach John Wooden. Wooden had a unique way of inspiring his players with his grounded approach to success. He shunned the limelight and encouraged his players to focus on being better people first, before being better players. Wooden taught his players to be the same in victory and in defeat: gracious. As a result, Wooden secured ten NCAA national championships in a 12-year period (including seven in a row), an untouchable feat.

Wooden, who passed away at the age of 99 in 2010, counseled, "Talent is God given, be humble; fame is man-given, be thankful; conceit is self-given, be careful." Good advice for life and for leadership.

Coaches and leaders who, like John Wooden, inspire and impact others see themselves as equal to, and choose to walk alongside, their people rather than in front of them. As you might guess, they earn admiration and respect from those they lead. Such leaders inspire others to buy into their vision of being both their best personal selves and their best organizational selves.

On the other hand, people are not usually inspired by leaders who think too much of themselves or who take advantage of their status or position. Leaders who lack humility try to impose their authority and power on others. Instead of building people up, they don't mind breaking them. How much time do you like spending around such people?

On a recent road trip, I listened to an interview with former Navy Seal Jay Hennessey. Jay was asked what differentiated the best and worst leaders. He replied, "I think it comes down to humility. Humility is the enabler for curiosity; it's the enabler for giving praise and showing appreciation for someone else. People without humility usually don't want to change their minds or go with a decision if it's not theirs." This, from a US Navy Seal who has both followed and led in countless life-and-death situations.

Carly Fiorina, CEO of HP from 1999-2005 and now a leadership expert, sees the dynamic between strength and humility. "Strength and confidence are necessary for leadership, but they must be balanced with humility. It is strength that pushes us forward in the face of difficulty. It is humility that keeps us open to course correction when required. It is strength that allows us to tackle the difficult problems. It is humility that reminds us others can help find solutions. It is strength that pushes us to ask the necessary, tough questions everyone fears. It is humility that allows us to hear the answers."

There are indeed times when a leader doesn't have all the answers. Acknowledging this and seeking input from others requires humility. Such leaders show respect for their people by acknowledging, listening and engaging with them. They value their team members' feedback and, in fact, have no problem sharing the limelight when successful.

American billionaire businessman and philanthropist David Rubenstein has this advice for younger people entering the workplace, "No matter how successful you become, don't let it go to your head. Maintain some humility." A former financial analyst, lawyer and co-executive chairman of American private equity firm The Carlyle Group, Rubenstein added that it's important for a leader to share the credit when success comes along.

Humble leaders have the confidence to recognize their own shortcomings. Rather than viewing their limits as a threat or a sign of frailty, they surround themselves with others who have complementary skills. In life, others will be more inspired by your imperfections and ability to overcome them than by your "perfections." Don't be afraid to show the imperfect side of yourself.

A fine case in point comes from James Kerr's book *Legacy*, which discusses the 15 principles of the mighty New Zealand All Blacks rugby team. One account about Coach Graham Henry is especially impressive and instructive. Team captain Tana Umaga asked Henry what he thought of his pre-game speeches. Henry, at first surprised by the question, replied that he thought his speeches were pretty good. Umaga, who was speaking on behalf of the whole team, suggested that maybe he should think about not doing them anymore. BOOM! Talk about feedback. Most coaches or leaders would have felt insulted, but Henry agreed and decided not to do them anymore. It takes a fair amount of humility for someone in a leadership position to do that. As you may guess if you are familiar with the success of the All Blacks, Henry's response lifted his players' respect for him even higher.

Leaders who have humility show appreciation for their people. More importantly, they will make a point of telling them often how grateful they are for them. They point out their strengths and qualities, knowing that people are more motivated and more inspired to work harder by encouragement rather than by criticism. Furthermore, leaders with humility elevate other people's greatness. They see others not just for who they are, but for who they can become. These leaders put others' needs before their own. Author C.S. Lewis famously observed, "Humility is not thinking less of yourself; it's thinking of yourself less." A good reminder of what true leadership is all about.

For the person in control, it's important to practice humility, not only to become a better leader, but, more importantly, to become a better person. Some people think that they can fake humility; they would be quite surprised by what people actually think of them. What's encouraging to know is that being humble is a skill that can be developed. Make the choice to become that better leader and that better person.

SELF-REFLECTION TIME

- As a leader, would you say that you have a high level of humility? Why? (These are not trick questions.)
- Describe what a leader with humility would look like to you.

"Humility is not thinking less of yourself, it's thinking of yourself less."

– C.S. Lewis

CHAPTER 35

Lead with Listening

The adage says, Listen and learn. There's a reason it doesn't say, *Talk* and learn. Andy Stanley, senior pastor at North Point Community Church, who has spent his career speaking, knows that failing to listen is risky. "Leaders who don't listen will eventually be surrounded by people who have nothing to say." Furthermore, if you won't listen to them, people who have valuable ideas to contribute will move on to organizations with leaders who will pay attention; those who remain in your organization will not be making a contribution.

Indeed, when you listen, you learn; but when you talk, you are merely repeating something you already know (or think you know). Coming from a sports coaching background, I have had the good fortune to work with some incredible world-class athletes. I learned that the more I listened, the more information I got from the athlete, which in turn helped me become a better coach.

In his book *The Seven Habits of Highly Effective People*, Stephen Covey explains this concept: "Seek first to understand, then to be understood," meaning "Listen well, before speaking." Covey believes that most people do not listen during conversations with others; instead, they rush to talk and to give advice or opinion. The reason is that people tend to relate what they hear to their own life experiences. This impedes their ability to properly understand or even consider other viewpoints.

A fine example of a great communicator and listener is the Scottish National rugby coach Gregor Townsend. Gregor, selected to play for his country 82 times, is one of the most humble and nicest guys I've ever met. I've been lucky enough to be invited to a few of the Scottish Rugby training sessions and pre-match days where I could see him interact with his players and fellow coaching staff. He is always locked in on them. He holds eye contact and lets others finish what they are saying. When they speak to Gregor, he is patient, and they know he is listening to them. For Gregor, paying attention has paid off.

Whether you are working with a single person or a large team, make it a point to listen in both individual and group capacities. Blair Cremin, the CEO at Stenhousemuir Football Club, recognizes the importance, for both coaches and leaders. "In leadership, perhaps the ability to listen separates the good from the great. People appreciate a conversation in which they feel acknowledged, heard and respected, and athletes are no different." He added that learning how to listen—really listen—is tough because the human tongue is "a beast few can master." A limited number of more precise words carries more weight than droning on. Furthermore, it is wise not to fill gaps or silences because it prevents the speaker from saying what they might be struggling to say.

The key is to start with the right mindset. Train yourself to keep quiet when others are speaking. Make it a habit to repeat back to them the gist of what they say to confirm their intent. Give thought to what they say. Ask open-ended questions—not yes or no questions, but ones that prompt the speaker to expand on what they are saying.

Great leaders know that they don't have all the answers and believe that the more they listen the more likely they are to have opportunities to make better decisions and find better solutions. These leaders value the feedback and opinions of their team members.

In a study of employee engagement, business advisor and best-selling author John Izzo found that the #1 reason team members and team employees don't take more initiative at their place of work is that their leaders fail to get their input and feedback before making decisions; that is, that they don't listen—or care to listen—to them. This is another reason why it's so important—for example, in meetings—to allow enough time for the team members to share their opinions and feedback.

Effective listeners don't listen only with their ears: they listen with all their senses. When they communicate with others, they are also aware of body language. They show that they are 100 percent focused on the other person by nodding and not letting distractions get in the way.

Communication Do's and Don'ts

Do

- Be aware of how much you talk in ratio to how much you listen when conversing with others.

- Stay present and eliminate any distractions that might draw your attention away from the person you are speaking with.

- Use positive body language. Remember that this, too, is a form of communication.

- Ask clarifying questions and repeat back what you have heard.

Don't

- Interrupt the other person.

- Assume you know all of the answers. Allow for the possibility that others have valuable information to share.

- React emotionally to what is being said. Acknowledge the information even if you don't agree with it.

- Look at your phone or let yourself become distracted.

SELF-REFLECTION TIME

- ◎ As a leader, how well do you listen to your team?
- ◎ Looking at the Do's and Don'ts, what areas do you feel you can improve in?

"Leaders who don't listen will eventually be surrounded by people who have nothing to say."

– Andy Stanley

CHAPTER 36

Lead with Feedback

F eedback—great leaders give respectfully and welcome it gladly. To paraphrase an old breakfast cereal motto, "Feedback is the breakfast of champions." To paraphrase a step further, feedback is the breakfast, lunch and dinner of champions.

Feedback can be divided into two categories: the kind you give and the kind you receive. And each of these can be divided into two categories: constructive and destructive. We should pay serious attention to the constructive and very little to the destructive. The better we learn to distinguish between the last two the better we become at the first two.

From birth we are accustomed to receiving feedback, but at some stage we tend to become defensive. One sure thing for leaders and team members alike, is that constructive feedback is what advances learning and improvement. Even though we might not always like what we hear, the more open we are to it, the faster and stronger we become.

Great leaders are skilled and generous at pointing out the positives of their team members and employees. They know that the highest form of motivation is praise—taking notice of what their people are doing and have done well. Positive feedback builds morale and self-confidence, and it boosts the likelihood of team success.

Providing happy news or positive feedback is easy; however, presenting the not-so-nice news in a constructive way is more challenging. Great leaders are just as competent at doing both supportively.

When great leaders deliver a negative assessment, they do it without condemning or shaming. A few years ago, when he was the Chelsea football manager, Jose Mourinho berated his physiotherapist, Eva Carneiro, live on television and to the world. Very soon after that, he left his position by mutual consent as other team members stepped forward to reveal that they, too, had been badly treated and berated.

In spite of being successful at winning trophies, Mourinho has a track record of falling out with clubs and people and having to move from one club to another. He later went on to manage rival clubs such as Manchester United 2016-2018 and Tottenham Hotspurs 2019-2021, both brief stints. Perhaps because he had been successful years earlier at clubs such as Chelsea, Real Madrid and Inter Milan, he didn't realize that today's generation of players doesn't respond favorably to his authoritarian style. It may have worked before, but times have changed. Simply put: Leaders and coaches who aren't willing to adapt the way they give feedback won't stay relevant.

Great leaders offer their feedback from a place of empathy. They focus more on solutions to the problem than on the person. Andy McKay, director of performance with the Seattle Mariners has been with the organization since 2015. When we talked, he expressed a strong opinion about this practice. "Leaders who are effective at providing feedback are best at shifting the focus of the conversation toward generating solutions and suggestions for improvement. They don't drift from this approach."

Team members and employees are motivated by leaders who care about them as people first. Leaders who have to deliver difficult feedback and have already established healthy relationships with their people usually get more favorable outcomes.

For providing feedback, I apply the acronym, **PPTT**. First have the conversation with the right **person** or people. Second, have it in the right **place**. For example, giving negative feedback or criticism in front of other people may not be the right place. Third, pay attention to the right **timing**. Finally, use the right **tone.** The way we say something can be received very differently if the tone of voice is wrong. Don't undermine your message.

Leaders are quite used to giving advice and offering feedback to their team members, fellow staff members or employees, but how many are open to receiving feedback from their team? When I was working as a sports performance coach, I liked to ask what I termed the most important question in coaching: "What do you think?" I asked athletes about how things were going and where they saw room for improvement. They knew that they were part of the decision making process—that they had the opportunity to deliver feedback and take ownership and accountability.

Are your team members able to offer feedback well? Do they have the freedom and ability to praise you for handling things well *and* to deliver negative feedback in constructive and empathetic ways? You establish and model your culture. That's why you're the leader. Effective leaders welcome feedback and are deeply interested in what their people are saying and how they are feeling. Foster a culture that promotes both giving and receiving feedback appropriately at all levels within your organization. It's up to you to lead by example. Soliciting feedback requires vulnerability and the confidence to hear and accept it. When team members see that their leader is open to it, they are more likely to accept and apply it themselves.

One easy way to get feedback is simply to ask for it—not demand it—in an appropriate time and place. You can start with specific questions like "What went well in that meeting or practice?" and "What would have made it better?" When your people see that you are paying attention to what they have said, they will be more comfortable giving less positive feedback. You reap two benefits here. First, you know that you have created a safe environment for team members to voice opinions. Second, you gain valuable ideas from the people you have chosen for your team.

7 Simple Tips for Receiving Feedback as a Leader

1. Ask the right people, not just the ones who will tell you what you want to hear.

2. Ask for feedback in the right setting.

3. Choose the appropriate time.

4. Use the appropriate tone.

5. Listen and don't interrupt, even if you don't agree with something.

6. Refrain from making inappropriate facial expressions or body language.

7. Smile and thank the person for the feedback.

8 Questions Leaders Can Ask People on Their Team or in Their Organization (Preferably in a One-on-one Meeting)

1. What is going well here?

2. What could be improved?

3. What challenges are you encountering right now?

4. What can I, as a leader, do better here?

5. If you were me, what would you do differently?

6. What one thing annoys you the most here and why?

7. How can I best support you?

8. What's the best thing about this organization?

Make giving and receiving constructive feedback the way of doing business in your organization.

SELF-REFLECTION TIME

- As a leader, where do you feel you could improve when providing criticism or feedback to others?

- As a leader, where do you feel you could improve when it comes to receiving criticism and feedback from others?

"Leaders who are effective at providing feedback are best at shifting the focus of the conversation toward generating solutions and suggestions for improvement. They don't drift from this approach."

– Andy McKay

CHAPTER 37

Lead with Empathy

In February 2020, just before the world was put into lockdown due to the COVID-19 pandemic, I was presenting at a leadership conference at the St. Georges Lower School for Girls in Edinburgh, Scotland.

On that particular morning, I was speaking on, among other things, emotional intelligence and the importance of having empathy and humility as a leader. As I was coming down from the stage following the first session, a gentleman approached me and asked if we could have a quick chat.

He had been struggling with something in the workplace for a while and wanted my opinion on the matter. He asked me if showing empathy toward his employees was a sign of weakness or frailty. He explained that he felt that when he showed empathy or compassion, some of his people took advantage of that. They saw his kindness as weakness. I completely understood his point of view. Unfortunately, the truth is yes, this can happen. However, I have always believed that those who take advantage of kind people are not the type of people I want in my organization. Also, I mentioned that it's sometimes good to be on guard with certain people and not be too open or show too much empathy. A leader, like all of us, must be aware that not everyone is going to be on our side or want the best for us.

In organizations where a healthy culture is in action, we see that empathy is demonstrated at the top and passed down throughout the organization. The reaffirming results are an increase in teamwork and a decrease in conflict and disruption. On the people side of the scale, this leads to a more positive work environment. On the numbers side of the scale, it leads to increased productivity. Win-win!

Leaders who have empathy usually have a high level of emotional intelligence. They have compassion and aim to better understand others' feelings and viewpoints. These leaders have a genuine interest in the lives of those they lead and take the time to learn about them. Scott Galloway, professor of marketing at the New York University Stern School of Business, and author of books such as *The Algebra of Happiness* and *Post Corona*, writes, "Empathy creates loyalty. You have to want others to win, and you have to leverage all of your talents to help others be a success." A point to remember: Their success is your success.

Great leadership is not only about professional interest but also about personal interest, and the strongest way to build them is through the building of relationships and making closer connections. In the work or professional environment, empathy allows leaders to better understand root causes behind poor performance or behaviors. After working in the sports world for a while, I realized that when an athlete was going through a slump in their performance level, the vast majority of the time it was not due to a lack of game skills, but rather something going on in their personal life that was affecting their confidence and belief systems.

Because of the way I was coached and taught as a kid, in the early years of my coaching career, I had far less empathy and patience than I do today. I was brought up in a very military-like and autocratic style of leadership, so if an athlete wasn't working hard in practice or not competing well, I would just put it down to their having a bad attitude or being lazy. And due to this approach, I was sometimes even tougher on them. Not surprisingly, I didn't get the results I intended.

Then one day I had a conversation with a youth coach who enlightened me on this subject. He told me about a kid on his team who had been acting strangely and aggressively toward his teammates. The kid had become disruptive and was upsetting some of the other kids on the team, behaviors that were out of character. The coach had scolded him a few times and even benched him for a few games for his behavior. After a few weeks, the coach approached the kid after practice, well away from the other kids, and asked what was going on. Within seconds, the kid's eyes welled up. He told the coach that his parents were in the middle of a divorce and things at home were extremely hostile and turbulent. The coach said that he learned a valuable lesson that day. Before we judge or come down hard on someone, we should know all the facts. There's a reason why people act the way they do.

Being empathetic allows leaders and coaches to help better understand behaviors and situations and to better deal with them. In addition, it allows them to build and develop stronger relationships with those they lead.

At its core, empathy is a vital component in leading others. It means getting out of one's own shoes and into someone else's to truly understand what is happening within and around them. It means being able to understand others' thoughts, feelings and needs and how all of these impact their perceptions and their performance. It doesn't mean that you have to agree with how they see things, but that you are willing and better able to understand what that other person is going through. Being empathetic gives you the knowledge of the true problem and the ability to handle it well: indeed, a win for everyone.

Cultivating empathy as a leadership skill lets you create bonds of trust. Start by being a good listener. Listen to really understand the other person, not just to hear them.

SELF-REFLECTION TIME

- ◎ As a leader, can you list one or two examples of when you showed empathy to someone you lead?

- ◎ Why do you think it's important for a leader to have empathy?

"Empathy creates loyalty. You have to want others to win, and you have to leverage all of your talents to help others be a success."

– Scott Galloway

CHAPTER 38

Lead with Competence

Those who lead well and make an impact in this world are those who are on a lifelong mission to grow and better themselves. Great leaders are always looking for ways to improve. They want to have—and be known for—their expertise. To stop learning, to stop improving mean stagnating and becoming yesterday's news.

We expect our leaders to have expertise in many areas, especially in the ones that affect the team and its potential for success. However, when you take a close look at most leaders, it becomes clear that those who actually have expertise are rare and that mediocrity is the norm. Unfortunately, incompetent leaders can be spotted all too often.

The people who follow you want to know that they can rely on you to have expertise in the important areas. They want to know they can lean on you in times of adversity. It's impossible to be competent in every area of leadership, but you must have talents and skills where it counts. Know your strengths and acknowledge your weaknesses. If you're great with motivating people and creating a positive environment, then maximize those strengths. If you're not great at leading meetings or you lack good organizational skills, work on them. The best competitive advantage you will ever have is *you*.

Because the person in charge cannot achieve distinction alone, they surround themselves with people who arc bcttcr in the areas where they fall short. To build a strong team, great leaders see other people's strengths as complements to their weaknesses, not as threats to their position of authority.

When I asked, Peter Goodyer, the CEO and headmaster at Bedes School in the South of England if his leadership style had changed over the years, he said, "Yes, for sure it's changed. I used to very much see the leader in a way that they were this all-conquering figure who had all the answers. But that is not how I see it in today's world. I see leadership as more about harnessing the strengths of those around me and creating the environment in which others are able to flourish and for their ideas and thoughts to be heard and acted upon."

Liverpool manager and head coach Jurgen Klopp addressed this topic. He said that he knows his shortcomings and purposely hires and surrounds himself with those who are stronger in the areas where he is not as strong. Learning from them improves his expertise.

Competent leaders build the knowledge, skills and experience to know who and what they need and how to make the most of what they have.

They

- Possess good people skills
- Foster a healthy culture
- Influence and impact others
- Find mutually beneficial solutions to problems
- Produce quality results

Great leaders have standards of excellence, and they are disciplined in maintaining them. Furthermore, these principles extend to all areas of their life, not just to their leadership responsibilities. Consistently going above and beyond what is expected sets the example of excellence for those who respect and look up to them.

Maintaining expertise requires lifelong learning. Instead of being trapped by yesterday's knowledge or stances, great leaders practice honest self-evaluation and seek new skills and information. Make this your approach to expertise, if it isn't already. You will enjoy payoffs, both professional and personal.

One way to make this a reality is by spending time with other great leaders who value these goals.

You can also

- Observe great leaders

- Read about leadership

- Watch videos and TED Talks of great leaders

- Take leadership courses

- Be open to feedback about your leadership style

SELF-REFLECTION TIME

- ◎ As a leader, what areas do you feel you could improve in?

- ◎ What areas are your strengths? Your weaknesses?

"By stretching yourself beyond your perceived level of confidence, you accelerate your development of competence."

– Michael J. Gelb

CHAPTER 39

Lead with Chemistry

As the saying goes, teamwork makes the dream work. Chemistry is what draws a group of individuals together as a team. Chemistry differs from collaboration in that collaboration is a conscious choice and chemistry is a gut-level bond. Motor car pioneer Henry Ford observed, "If everyone is moving forward together, then success takes care of itself." Think of any winning sports team or thriving organization—what are the chances that they don't have a great team chemistry?

Chemistry is a group dynamic that occurs when members of the team work together to accomplish mutual goals. When the group starts to meet them, chemistry builds, sparking more success: an upward spiral. It is the leader's responsibility to create the environment that facilitates this dynamic.

Positive chemistry greatly increases the chances of achieving excellence in a team environment. Leaders who focus on building it within their organizations have usually gathered together various personalities who are energized and want to work collaboratively. This approach matches one of Golden State Warriors coach Steve Kerr's: Chemistry in a team is more about the "we" than the "me." As I mentioned earlier, Kerr is such a strong believer in the power of team chemistry that he sometimes hands coaching and decision making over to the players.

Among the many great team cultures I've been involved with, nearly all of them had a great aura of team chemistry. Sure, they had their challenges and problems, just like any other team or organization, but by maintaining a healthy togetherness and team chemistry, they were able to address issues and challenges more quickly and with more favorable outcomes.

We looked at this question before, but it applies here as well: How many times have you seen great sports teams loaded with an array of superstars and talented individuals that for some reason could never realize their full potential? Babe Ruth, one of major league baseball's hottest home run hitters of all time, reportedly once noted, "You may have the greatest bunch of individual stars in the world, but if they don't play together, the club won't be worth a dime."

Without chemistry, talented teams have a hard time functioning well. But with it, their people can cultivate and maximize each other's talents and skills. An example of failed team chemistry that often springs to mind is the England Football team of the early 2000 era. It featured incredible players such as David Beckham, Michael Owen, Paul Scholes and many more. On paper, it was a squad that most pundits felt should have won at least one world cup and many more international tournaments. But they underachieved horribly.

England team members Frank Lampard and Rio Ferdinand later said that they didn't fail due to a lack of skills or talent, but regrettably due to a lack of team chemistry. The squad was composed of players from different clubs—rival clubs. Lampard and Ferdinand agreed that because of such a strong rivalry between the clubs (predominantly Liverpool, Chelsea and Manchester United), the players chose to stick with their fellow club teammates during international duties rather than the new players they were temporarily teamed up with. This resulted in a divided team.

One of the greatest, most admirable managers and leaders in modern English football is Jurgen Klopp. The eccentric German, who stands over 6'4", took the English club Liverpool from contenders to champions in just 4 years. The team had been close numerous times to winning the Premiership title, but it was Klopp who built the team around a chemistry and togetherness that led them to their sixth Champions League title in 2019 and the Premier League title in 2020, their first in over 30 years.

During his 4-year tenure, Jurgen masterfully, one by one, let go of the people who didn't fit the vision of the club and brought in those who matched what he needed. He built the squad into a cohesive working unit. Like Klopp, great leaders know that it's not just about skill level, but perhaps even more about unity.

Teams that are having fun together are usually winning teams. When there is a leadership style present that promotes relationship building and encourages collaboration, there will be energy and solidarity. Happy and motivated team members are more committed and enthusiastic performers. They are not only people who execute well against the competition, they are also a group who enjoy being in each other's company and enjoy team chemistry.

Successful leaders have a focus on building teams that can work well together. Chemistry is key!

SELF-REFLECTION TIME

- ◎ As a leader, how would you describe the chemistry within your organization or team right now?

- ◎ Think of a team or organization that has (or had) a great team chemistry. What are some of the characteristics you recognized?

"If you want special results, you have to feel special things and do special things together.
You can speak about spirit, or you can live it."

– Jurgen Klopp

CHAPTER 40

Lead with Appreciation

Did you know that the main reason the majority of Americans leave their jobs isn't the number of vacation days they receive? Surprisingly, it isn't the desire for a higher paycheck, casual Friday, ping pong table, free donuts, or beanbags in the staff room. According to a Gallup poll of American workers, the number one reason why Americans leave their jobs is due to a lack of appreciation!

In fact, Gallup found that 65 percent of people feel underappreciated at work. In such a workplace environment, there will be low morale and negativity. These carry with them the baggage of limited engagement, low motivation and a lack of a buy-in. People want to know that their work matters; otherwise, they feel it is purposeless, and productivity plummets.

So, what does appreciation in the workplace look like? When I posed this question to a few leaders in my circle, typical replies were "being mindful of the effort and work others are doing" and "recognizing the contributions of others."

One of those leaders was the managing director of Brother UK, Phil Jones MBE. Over dinner one evening in Manchester, I asked Phil why he felt that appreciation in the workplace is so important. He replied, "When people know their contribution has made a difference in their workplace, it fuels satisfaction and often unlocks vital discretionary effort. It can cost nothing yet has an extraordinary lifting impact on the individual receiving honestly given positive feedback." He added, "If you want an individual or team to go beyond, then let them know, with specificity, where their value lies. As William Makepeace Thackeray said, 'Next to excellence is the appreciation of it.'"

A great example of showing appreciation is Pep Guardiola, manager and coach of the English football club Manchester City. After Manchester claimed the premiership title in 2020, Guardiola thanked all the Manchester City players and staff for achieving something he would cherish for the rest of his life. In fact, he gathered all of the people who worked for the club together to express his gratitude.

When those in charge lead with appreciation, they stay aware of what is happening around them by placing a focus on the small daily wins, what I term "process victories." For example, instead of complimenting a project only when it's completed or a target only when it's reached, smart leaders compliment the small achievements along the way.

Another strategy used by great leaders is that they look for "winning moments," a term I first heard of from Tony Strudwick, former Manchester United Football's Head of Performance. Winning moments are opportunities to tell a team member or colleague that they did something well and that it was greatly appreciated. What's more, great leaders know to praise the positives in public, and if they need to criticize, to do that in private.

Small but significant signs of gratitude keep the team engaged, motivated and inspired to continue to do great work.

Recognizing and telling others that they are appreciated is undoubtedly one of the most powerful forms of inspiration and motivation. When team members know that their efforts are recognized and appreciated, they feel that they are valued not just for their work, but, more importantly, they are valued as individuals.

It's not complicated. Simply say, "Thank you" for a job well done, or send an email or note expressing your feelings. Expressions of appreciation may cost a lot or may cost nothing, but for the recipient they are priceless. As leadership author and speaker Zig Ziglar said, "You never know when a moment and a few sincere words can have an impact on a life." Make having a positive impact on the lives of others part of your legacy.

SELF-REFLECTION TIME

- As a leader, how good are you at recognizing the efforts of your people and telling them? When was the last time?

- Why do you think it's important to recognize the efforts of your people?

"If you want an individual or team to go beyond, then let them know, with specificity, where their value lies."

– Phil Jones MBE

CHAPTER 41

Lead with Energy

When you're in the coaching, teaching, managing or leadership business, you are in the health and energy business. If you don't have the right level of energy, you can't expect to be an effective leader. You can't give what you don't have. If you are not taking care of your health and well-being, then you can't expect to lead others the way you would like to. Taking care of others, starts by first taking care of yourself.

Author and speaker Anthony Robbins lists the common traits of successful leaders he's worked with over the years. A key attribute is energy. Robbins says that many people fail to achieve what they want simply because the mind is willing, but the body is weak. Their mind says, "Let's go get 'em" and their body says, "I can't even get out of bed." This may be a bit of an overstatement, but you may be all too familiar with his point. Countless people, including leaders, are working while tired—on a regular basis.

Our health and energy are foundational to our lives—relationships, careers and quality. Unfortunately, real leadership, as we know it, is about putting others' (staffs', customers', clients', families' and friends') needs first, but it doesn't come without a price.

Leaders, more than most, are vulnerable to burnout, a condition in which being overworked turns into sheer exhaustion. Your goals, both professional and personal, are higher than most. You demand more of yourself in order to serve others better. You try to be the right example, do the right things and lead with confidence; however, that can take a toll on your well-being. On top of that, you have families and other people who are dependent on you. It's a lot to handle.

Of the many leaders and coaches I've worked with, I am sorry to say that more than 40 percent of them were burned out or getting close. Yes, the number is that high! The signs are easy to spot. You know you're heading for burnout when you are struggling to motivate even yourself, never mind others. You know you're heading for burnout when you are becoming more and more short tempered or impatient with others. You know you are heading for burnout when you are lacking creativity and joy in what you are doing.

This may sound selfish, but the truth is this: Your health and well-being come first. It's very much the same as when you are on an airplane and the flight attendant announces, "In case of a cabin pressure emergency, please put on your own mask first before assisting others." It's a simple concept that makes sense because you can't help others if you aren't in good shape yourself.

In 2017 Whole Foods CEO John Mackey sold the company to Amazon's Jeff Bezos for $13.7 billion. When asked what determines excellence in one's life, without pause he cited energy. Mackey believes that if you don't take care of your energy, meaning how you take care of your body and mind, it is absolutely impossible to achieve excellence in any area. Energy is essential to succeed at the highest level in any sector.

Seeing you take care of yourself provides your team both motivation and permission to pay attention to their own health—hugely beneficial to you. When your people are in good health, they miss fewer days of work, are in better physical health when they arrive and are in a more positive frame of mind when they work.

I am a strong believer in the importance of a consistent morning routine, as you may know if you have read any of my other books. Having a morning routine helps prime your mind and body for the day ahead and sets you up for both short-term and long-term success.

My morning routine includes 20 minutes of exercise, 20 minutes of reading and 20 minutes of thoughtfulness (thinking of others and texting them a message, whether it's "good luck," "get well" or something else. I also have a good breakfast before starting my day. It is fuel for the brain and the body. Just as with a car, if you are low on fuel, you aren't going to get very far. If you don't have a morning routine already, I strongly encourage you to design one that works for you, even if it's for only 20 minutes.

Because of the nature of my work, I am lucky that I can usually get in a 20-minute nap after lunch—again, I hope you can find a way to work this into your routine. It allows me to re-charge for the remainder of the day. I also pay attention to staying hydrated. All living things need that! Low energy = low performance and low focus.

To lead with energy, you first need to establish a plan that motivates you to act. The leaders who are most successful at maintaining their mental and physical health are those who set aside time for exercise, establish personal boundaries that allow them to rest and recover well, find creative ways to eat healthy meals and stay hydrated. You have to be intentional. Much the same as having a plan for leading your people, have a plan for leading your health and safety.

The most important appointment of the day is with yourself. And if you aren't keeping it, you're never going to be able to get the best out of yourself and those you lead. It's not being selfish. Remember: Leaders who pay attention to their health and energy set the example for the others on the team to follow.

SELF-REFLECTION TIME

- ◎ As a leader, list 3 ways you could raise your energy levels.

- ◎ List 3 advantages of having a great energy.

"The most important appointment of the day is with yourself."

– Allistair McCaw

CHAPTER 42

Lead with Heart

Mike Krzyzewski, the legendary head basketball coach at Duke University and a USA Olympic basketball coach wrote one of my favorite books on leadership, *Leading with the Heart*, in which he discusses the importance of having your heart in the right place. He explains that unless you are willing to lead with an authentically positive heart, people won't buy into you either as a leader or as a person, and he defines authenticity as living a life that is strongly connected to one's belief system. When you are authentic, it's obvious that you are living up to your values, whatever they are.

Mac Anderson, speaker and author of many motivational books, writes that great leadership most often starts with "a willing heart, a positive attitude, and a desire to make a difference." This pretty much sums up Coach K. If you have seen Coach K on the court, you know that he's fired up, sometimes loud and always passionate.

The members of Coach K's team—and everyone else—trust in what he does on and off the court. If he doesn't like what you're doing, he'll tell you. What's more, Coach K will openly admit that he doesn't always get it right. He is honest and secure enough to acknowledge his mistakes. How do his players respond to a coach who admits mistakes? Check out his stunning lifetime coaching stats: 1157-350 overall record and five national championships through the 2020 season. His players have faith in him, and they want to live up to his faith in them.

Those who genuinely lead with their heart and not just their head are more equipped to connect with the emotional needs of their team members and with employees who know they are valued, listened to, included—and respected. When you support your people through their personal challenges and difficulties, you not only show heart, you win hearts. People feel more motivated to work harder and give their all for you. People don't work for organizations; they work for their leader.

Leading with heart draws together many other leadership qualities. Compassion, collaboration, engagement, and honesty are integral to people with this dedication. And appropriately, they reap the benefits. What they do for their people sets the example for behavior toward each other and back toward their leader. It ultimately serves the common good and the goals of the organization.

For over 40 years at Duke University, Coach K has been able to form deep and meaningful relationships with his players season after season, so that each group becomes a family. In fact, when I was visiting with him in his office, he shared with me that part of his recruiting formula is this: When he is considering a player to recruit, that player must first meet with Coach K's family over dinner. It's a family decision, not just his.

When you lead with your heart and touch the hearts of your people, they will remember: They might not remember what you said, but they will always remember how you made them feel. And this feeling, the one that emanates from your heart and warms their hearts, unleashes the full power and creativity of individuals and teams.

Leading with heart is about being fully invested in your people. As you can tell, Coach K's players and staff know he cares deeply about them and that he wants to see them succeed not only in basketball, but in the game of life. When your people know that you genuinely care about them, they will work to succeed for themselves and for you. You win, your people win and your organization wins.

SELF-REFLECTION TIME

- ◎ As a leader, how do you lead from the heart?
- ◎ In what ways do you feel you could do better?

"A common mistake among those who work in sports is spending a disproportional amount of time on the X's and O's as compared to time spent learning about people."

– Mike Krzyzewski

CHAPTER 43

Lead with Non-negotiables

E ven though we talk a lot about the importance of being adaptable as a leader, there are also matters that must be dealt with more firmly. They are the non-negotiables.

Non-negotiables are principles that cannot be compromised on, either for yourself or your team members. They are there to guide you through hard times when decision making is difficult. These values define not only what you expect and won't accept from others, but also what you expect and won't accept from yourself. They are the promises you keep to everyone.

Being firm and consistent in the non-negotiables is critical to building trust and respect from those you lead. If there are double standards in areas where the leaders or team members are allowed to bend the "rules," it can have a detrimental effect on your reputation and on the health of the organization.

Leaders of cultures of excellence know that there's value in remaining open-minded and adaptable in areas such as, strategy, planning and decision making. However, perhaps more important is standing firm in non-negotiables such as values, ethics and standards.

Moreover, having a clear set of expectations for yourself enables you to make decisions that are better for your own professional growth and career path. It provides you with a personal framework to adhere to and measure your own contributions by.

Let's look at a few examples of non-negotiables of some of the world's highest performers and leaders in their fields. For Toto

Wolff, head of Mercedes Benz F1 team, non-negotiables include honesty and authenticity. Brad Stevens, head coach of the Boston Celtics, identifies commitment and work ethic as his non-negotiables. Steph Houghton, captain of the England Women's football team, requires punctuality and respect for others.

Maybe you noticed three paragraphs up that I mentioned the word "rules" in quotation marks. Please note: Standards far outweigh rules. When there are rules in an organization, you will find less buy-in from its people. The word "rules" itself implies that they are coming from the leader, and that they are the leader's rules. One person's rules can be arbitrary and may seem to allow people more leeway to break them. However, when there are standards in place that are organizational or have been decided on or agreed to by the group, there will be more collective buy-in and accountability. Standards cannot be compromised.

Several years ago, I put together a list of standards and non-negotiables for leaders, organizations and teams to consider adopting. Whatever they choose creates total clarity about what is expected from everyone. It is essential to be unambiguous from the beginning with prospective employees about fixed expectations. Before taking a new person into your organization, clearly communicate your non-negotiables—leave no room for misunderstandings. Without full disclosure from day one, vague expectations give people leeway to set their own rules. Mayhem is a logical consequence.

Here are some non-negotiables for your organization to consider:

- Attitude
- Commitment
- Communication
- Dress code
- Honesty
- Humility (absence of ego)
- Integrity

- Positive attitude
- Punctuality
- Resolved conflict
- Respect
- Upholding core values
- Teamwork
- Work Ethic

There can't be two sets of non-negotiables within an organization: There is one for everyone, regardless of rank, position or status. Great teams have them. Great leaders live them and enforce them.

SELF-REFLECTION TIME

- ◎ As a leader, what are your non-negotiables?

- ◎ When was the last time a non-negotiable was violated within your organization? What was it and how did you address it?

"We are building a culture of accountability, trust and togetherness. Entitlement will not be tolerated."

– Brad Stevens

CHAPTER 44

Lead with Impact

Great leadership starts with influence, which, when well received, develops into impact.

University of Kentucky head basketball coach John Calipari was Atlantic 10 Coach of the Year three times, Naismith College Coach of the Year three times and is a Hall of Famer. He knows something about influence and impact. Calipari said, "Leadership is about impact. If you want to have an impact on someone, they first must want to be influenced by you." Many lucky young men have been both influenced and impacted under Calipari's direction.

Another basketball great was Kobe Bryant. During an incredible NBA career that spanned 20 seasons, Bryant won 5 championships and earned an NBA record 15 selections for All-NBA teams and 12 for All-Defensive teams. He won his Season MVP in 2007-08 and the Finals MVP in the next two years, and the list of his basketball achievements goes on. Although not everyone was a fan of Kobe's demanding style, he set the example by consistently demanding the most from himself. As an athlete, Kobe was superb, and without a doubt he will go down as one of the greatest who ever played the game.

However, it wasn't only his feats on the basketball court that set Kobe apart. He was also a highly respected human being and leader off the court. It was evident in how he spoke about his family, his teammates and his coaching staff, and in the topics he spoke to the media about. Kobe and his wife founded the Kobe and Vanessa Bryant Family Foundation and made large contributions to the Make-a-Wish Foundation, Boys and Girls Clubs, and other charities that supply kids with food, sports opportunities and scholarships. Furthermore, he generously devoted time and resources to charities around the world.

Kobe wanted to set the example as the hardest working player on the court, to maintain high standards and to live with wholehearted enthusiasm for his many and varied commitments. Kobe earned the respect and trust of those he led—and of those who looked up to him from a distance. He impacted people from his high school basketball court to around the world. In early 2020, when Kobe was tragically killed along with eight others in a helicopter crash near his home in Calabasas, California, we lost a great ambassador of the game and of life.

As you might guess, I read and study a lot about leadership. I especially enjoy the work of Dan Black, a leadership expert and author of the book *The Leadership Mandate*. Dan identifies four types of influence a leader can have: negative, neutral, positive, and life changing.

Leaders who exert negative influence are the most damaging. They focus on their authority, power, or title and are often egocentric and prideful. Their influence leaves the team or organization impacted in a very bad way. Dan recommends that we avoid people who choose to treat others this way.

Leaders with the second type, neutral influence, neither add to nor take away from what others are doing. In a group of people, they would not necessarily do anything that would cause them to stand out or be seen as a leader; they don't proactively lead or take charge. These people may be in leadership positions, but they are not actually leaders. Obviously, Dan recommends that we avoid people with these first two types of influence.

Leaders with the third type, positive influence, add value and leave the people they come in contact with better off as a result of their actions and attitude. They actively lead, build relationships with others, and are present in the effort to inspire, coach, and lead people to produce better results. They want to make a positive impact in the lives of those they lead and help them to be successful in all areas of their life.

Leaders with the final type, life-changing influence, are among the few people who possess the reach of this level of influence. It takes years or even decades of leading well and with positive influence to attain life-changing influence status. Life changing influence is about impact—impacting in a way that lives are permanently improved. People like Thomas Edison, Henry Ford, John Calipari and Kobe Bryant exerted this kind of influence, which betters the lives of countless people long after they are gone.

The ability to lead with purpose and make an impact should be every leader's primary goal. First you formulate your purpose. Then you make personal connections that help you decide who will be on your team. When you form deeper relationships with the people you have chosen, you will earn their trust and the right to influence them. As they get to know your integrity better, they will then allow you to have an impact on them.

Leaders have an incredible opportunity—and responsibility—to impact the lives of those they lead. Projects come and go, organizations rise and fall, people enter and depart, but the impact you leave on others lasts down through the generations.

SELF-REFLECTION TIME

- As a leader, in what ways do you feel you are making an impact?

- What role model leaders do you see making a positive impact today? What lessons can be learned from colleagues at the top of their game?

"Leadership is about impact.
If you want to have an impact on someone,
they first must want to be influenced by you."

– John Calipari

Differences between a Poor Leader and a Great Leader

Poor Leader	Great Leader
Generates fear	Inspires enthusiasm
Says "I"	Says "We"
Places blame on others	Takes responsibility
Is fixed minded	Is growth minded
Uses people	Develops people
Takes credit	Gives credit
Commands	Asks
Criticizes	Compliments
Puts others down	Empowers others

Conclusion

You, too, can be the great leader others will remember in the years to come.

Consider your present skill set and how the 44 lessons can help you rise to the level of greatness. You are the most important person you will ever lead. Approach honing your abilities with determination and perseverance. The payoff is becoming a better version of yourself every day.

Live the high standards you set for your people. Build relationships with them, earn their trust—and they will allow you to influence and then to have an impact on their lives.

Keep this book handy, open it randomly, and reflect again on the end-of-chapter questions. Remember the examples and wise words of the standouts who are successful and respected enough to be recognized and quoted. Like them, be positive, be inspiring.

What legacy do you want to leave? When people hear your name, what do you want them to say about you? Live your life so that they will speak with admiration not only about the great leader who achieved their goals, but also about how you made them feel, how you helped them grow, how you instilled self-belief in them and how you empowered them to become exceptional in whatever field they chose.

You have an incredible opportunity to realize your purpose and to make a positive and lasting impact on those you lead every day. Seize it.

Lead with Purpose

Workshop

Refine your skills in order to
Lead with Purpose and Make a Lasting Impact.

Now that you've read the book, take the opportunity to invite Allistair to personally work with you and your team!

These workshops are tailored to suit the client and their needs.

All workshops also include a discounted rate on bulk orders for books shipped within the continental U.S.A.

To find out more please email info@allistairmccaw.com

To view a sample of Allistair and his work, check out: https://www.youtube.com/watch?v=QCbfOFXZizE

Allistair is also an internationally acclaimed
keynote speaker and has spoken in
over 50 countries around the globe.

Some of the topics he speaks on include:
- Leadership
- Team & Organizational Culture
- Being Champion Minded

For booking enquiries, please e-mail:
info@allistairmccaw.com

Follow Allistair on social media:
Twitter: @allistairmccaw
Instagram: @bechampionminded
www.AllistairMccaw.com

All books available on Amazon.com

Hashtag on all social media: *#LeadWithPurpose*

About Denise McCabe

Denise McCabe is a freelance nonfiction editor. She has been helping writers shape, polish, and perfect their writing since 2002. Denise also develops and facilitates seminars in business writing and email effectiveness.

DENISE WORKS WITH

- Authors / Subject matter experts
- Corporations
- Government agencies
- Associations
- Educational institutions
- Banking institutions

For more details, please contact

denise@mccabeediting.com

www.MccabeEditing.com

Printed in Great Britain
by Amazon

79469089R00122